MEMOIRS *of an* ADHD MIND

MEMOIRS
of an
ADHD MIND

God was a Genius in the Way He Made Me

Melissa Hood

New York

MEMOIRS *of an* ADHD MIND
God was a Genius in the Way He Made Me

© 2015 **Melissa Hood**.

Published in New York, New York, by Morgan James Publishing. Morgan James and The Entrepreneurial Publisher are trademarks of Morgan James, LLC. www.MorganJamesPublishing.com

The Morgan James Speakers Group can bring authors to your live event. For more information or to book an event visit The Morgan James Speakers Group at www.TheMorganJamesSpeakersGroup.com.

A free **eBook** edition is available
with the purchase of this print book.

CLEARLY PRINT YOUR NAME ABOVE IN UPPER CASE

Instructions to claim your free eBook edition:
1. Download the BitLit app for Android or iOS
2. Write your name in **UPPER CASE** on the line
3. Use the BitLit app to submit a photo
4. Download your eBook to any device

ISBN 978-1-63047-480-5 paperback
ISBN 978-1-63047-482-9 eBook
ISBN 978-1-63047-481-2 hardcover
Library of Congress Control Number:
2015902156

Cover Design by:
Chris Treccani
www.3dogdesign.net

Interior Design by:
Bonnie Bushman
bonnie@caboodlegraphics.com

In an effort to support local communities and raise awareness and funds, Morgan James Publishing donates a percentage of all book sales for the life of each book to Habitat for Humanity Peninsula and Greater Williamsburg

Get involved today, visit
www.MorganJamesBuilds.com

Habitat
for Humanity®
Peninsula and
Greater Williamsburg
Building Partner

TABLE OF CONTENTS

THANK YOU

I wanted to use this page to thank my mom for all her love, support, and encouragement and for always showing me what love is through her actions. You have expressed God's love to me in a way that has aided me in becoming who God and Jesus meant for me to be. Thank you for your sacrifice during times that, as a single parent, I know must have been difficult, especially when you were trying to deal with your own hurts. I can never tell you of my gratitude for pushing me into the arena that I dreamed about because you believed!

Thank you for seeing my potential through this condition, a condition that has brought me much frustration and heartache, but in the end has taught me more about me than any lesson in life ever could. I love you Mom—I love you and Dad for teaching me to persevere and that I really could do ANYTHING in this life that I set my heart and mind to.

viii | MEMOIRS *of an* ADHD MIND

Also—for the readers—all the names in this book have been changed but my own, out of respect for those who might want to keep their identities private.

I would also like to suggest that you read only one chapter per sitting. There is a lot of "meat" in each chapter, and these breaks in your reading will enable you to retain more of the information. The format of the book takes you back into my past and then brings you forward to my present and my current insights into ADHD and how it has and does affect me.

Moving forward!

Foreword

by Omar S. López, PhD

What is it like to live with Attention Deficit Disorder (ADD) or Attention Deficit Hyperactivity Disorder (ADHD)? How does one cope with these conditions while meeting the demands of school, work, and family? When life seems too complicated, confusing, and overwhelming, where does one with ADD or ADHD go for understanding and support? How do parents, siblings, and others create the right environment where children and adults with ADD or ADHD succeed in living a purposeful life?

If you, a friend, or someone in your family has ADD or ADHD and are seeking further insights into how to overcome these conditions, then Missy Hood's, *Memoirs of an ADHD Mind* is a book you need to read and reference often.

I first met Missy when she was a graduate student at Texas State University where she earned a Master of Arts in Interdisciplinary Studies. As part of her program requirements, Missy completed a fifteen-month research study on college students with ADHD and their coping strategies that result in personal, academic, and professional success. Yes, people like Missy with ADHD do achieve high levels of achievement beyond what many people believe is possible!

This book is about how that achievement happens. Missy begins your journey to understanding the world of ADD and ADHD with her life story of how she was a nondiagnosed ADHD child and how this played out as she struggled through school. Here, the reader will benefit greatly from Missy's authentic accounts of living in the ADD/ADHD world— giving parents and guardians, as well as educators, insights into the emotional, physical, and psychological needs of young ADHD children relevant to their success at home, school, and the community. Through Missy's own experiences, you will then examine the ADHD life as a teenager and young adult, where you will appreciate the ADHD challenges to child and adult development.

At this point in the reading, Missy has established for the reader a solid grasp of ADHD from her own experience coping with the condition, and then begins to develop the vision described in the second part of the book's title: *God was a genius in the way He made me.*

I personally find this aspect of Missy's book appealing because I observe consistently in my own work helping others in life planning that people's ability to cope with personal challenges is highly dependent on their strength of character when based on some spiritual context. In this regard, Missy does not see ADHD as a "curse" but rather as a "condition to overcome" knowing that God's blueprint for her life was perfect.

The reader will be spellbound throughout the remaining book chapters as Missy continues to share stories of her life odyssey with ADHD, describing the coping interventions and insights acquired for success within this spiritual context. In so doing, Missy seeks to inspire you to help yourself or others with ADHD achieve higher levels of personal, academic, and professional success. This is part of her purposeful life—to inspire others to achieve great things despite ADD or ADHD.

If that too is what you seek for yourself or others, then this book is for you.

I leave the reader with my final insight as I reflect about Missy as a person: by giving of yourself to help others to overcome ADD or ADHD, you transcended your ADHD from a "condition to overcome" to a "gift to others."

Yes, Missy. God was a genius in the way He made you.

—Omar S. López, PhD

Chapter 1

MY CHILDHOOD
Being a Nondiagnosed ADHD Child—
Impulsivity and Hyperactivity

Taping my hair back on probably wasn't the brightest idea I had ever come up with, but at ten years old—hey, what's a kid to do? I had just cut my bangs, and there was a huge gash in them that was absolutely not hideable. My mother was going to kill me so I came up with the ultimate solution: why not tape them back on? She'd never notice and they would have time to grow back out. I stood in front of the mirror looking at my new idea with optimism but also a kind of dread, knowing inside that my mother (the detailed-oriented woman that she was and is) was somehow going to find out about my master plan.

1

This was my mentality as a child, a nondiagnosed ADHD child. I was always finding myself in predicaments that others around me seemed to frown upon. My poor mom! I kept her busy night and day with my constant hyperactivity, while others (relatives, family friends) dreaded my presence because of my need to always be in action.

This wasn't completely my fault, though I didn't know that then. The science world had yet to discover the so-called "condition" of ADHD (Attention Deficit Hyperactivity Disorder). To me, in my family, I was just being a goofy, mischievous kid trying my best to get through this thing called life.

Growing up wasn't easy for me. I was a tomboy, raised in a military family, where everything and everyone had to be in its place. Except for me, of course. Everything in my life seemed out of place—until my mother got a hold of me. She was always trying to make me into the little girl I should have been. But deep within me, there was this constant flurry of activity building. It was like I knew something big was supposed to happen through my life, but I didn't know how to get it here except to make it happen myself.

Adventure was my middle name, and if things seemed stagnant, well, I was fixing to get them stirred up the minute I walked into the room. In my opinion, if life wasn't exciting, it was my job to make it that way by the time I left. "Leave no stone unturned" was my motto. Needless to say, for all the calm people in my family, this was a challenge. I continually kept them on their toes. The second my feet hit the ground, I was running carelessly all over the place, knocking things over or breaking things, whether at home or in department stores. Life just wasn't the same for me unless something was happening for good or bad. (She writes this as she cringes.)

My mom was always the more laid back one of my parents. The minute my father walked into a room, if you were out of order, you knew you were in big trouble. He really was a big rough-tough cream puff, and I knew deep in my heart that he loved me. I actually was and am still very close to my mom, especially after my father died when I was twenty-two. His death would be the eye-opener to my condition. I would later learn that his military background had actually helped to keep the undiagnosed ADHD in check. His required order wasn't easy for me to maintain because in my world of ADHD I lived in constant chaos. I didn't mean to be disorderly, but my brain (unbeknownst to my parents) was misfiring, causing impulsivity, which would later lead to my bad choices and land me in places we never meant for me to land.

You see, you have to understand the ADHD mind: the brain with ADHD is wired differently from birth. The normal brain of a child understands when their parent tells them that the stove is hot and says "Don't touch." A normal child would heed the warning and probably go find something safer to do. My brain listened to the command, but impulsivity and curiosity would take over and I just had to touch the stove to see if what they told me was really the truth. The end result on one occasion was a huge blister that took two weeks to heal and a lot of pain and scolding for not listening.

ADHD children are notorious for hearing commands and then being impulsive and doing the opposite of what they are told. This in turn is misunderstood by the adults around them, and they are seen as disobedient or defiant. It's not like these kids mean to disobey; they just don't have any understanding of actions and consequences. Impulsivity really does work like that. My actions were always seen as mischievous, but were driven by this need to know. I never was one to take people at their words, well, except when I was older and had learned to master the impulsivity. I wasn't mean-spirited, or meaning to get into trouble, it just kind of happened. Impulsivity is a powerful force within ADHD kids. I believe until it is mastered it drives ADHD children with a need to experience life for themselves. As a child, I never meant to disobey. I just meant to live life to the fullest until it overflowed, and that sometimes landed me in hot water.

There were times when my impulsivity could really make my parents angry. Once we were out at my Grandma Mae's house in Taylor, Texas, and my mother had distinctly told me NOT to play with the matches. My grandparents lived in a little two-story upstairs garage apartment. Somehow I managed to drape strips of toilet paper over the towel hanger in the bathroom and light the strips on fire. I did this because of my curiosity and boredom and the impulsivity that drove me to act. I never considered that I could burn the entire house down. I was quickly caught by my mother, who frantically put out my strips of ignited toilet paper right before the flame hit the bottom hem of the window curtains. I write this rolling my eyes and asking, "Oh my God, what was I thinking?"

Did your parents ever ask you those words, "WHAT WERE YOU THINKING?!" Well, mine did all the time, so much so that I lost track of the motive behind the words. To me my curiosity was the driving force behind my actions, but I didn't know how to explain myself let alone what I did.

The ultimate test came for my mother when I was in fifth grade. I had landed myself in the principal's office because I had coaxed a classmate (named Carl Lehman) through the window of our classroom. I had had a crush on Carl for two years, and this was my ultimate expression of love. I told him, "It's OK, just climb on through." I gave little thought to the possibility that he might trip. In fact, the minute his left foot touched the floor, his entire body flew forward and hit the bookcase. This flying-forward action would prove to be my downfall as his body hit Mrs. Killibrew's bookcase with all of her European crystal on top. The inertia of his weight then caused it to tip (ever so slightly to the right), forcing it to completely fall over. I mean, how was I to know, that Carl's actions were going to knock over Mrs. Killibrew's crystal, along with all her teaching books, etc., into a heap on the floor? The look on her face as she whisked around the classroom door was enough to make any fifth grader fearful of their life. I looked up to see her beehive hairdo. As I let my eyes slowly make their way down to meet hers, I instantly saw her expression turn from shock to anger. That very moment I knew I was in for a long, hard year.

It proved to be a very hard year indeed. I would find myself getting blamed for many, many other things that I did not do because I was now on Mrs. Killibrew's radar. I thought she hated me. Along with constantly sending me to the principal's office, she would ridicule me or ask me to stay after school. My "stays" after school usually entailed her sitting in a chair in front of me asking me various questions that all led to one question: "Was I being abused at home?" I wasn't being abused at home, but I sure felt I was being abused at school with all of her crazy antics in response to my need to interact with my environment. My parents had always been very loving to me, and they showed it through their actions, so I never paid attention to Mrs. Killibrew's questioning. I was just behaving as the ADHD child that I was, and unfortunately, the condition hadn't been diagnosed yet. Lucky her, huh?

When I walked into Principal Sandoval's office on the morning that I invited Carl Lehman to climb through the window, she peered over her glasses and asked me why I was there. I sheepishly told her of my predicament, and she immediately looked away. I could have sworn she was trying super hard to keep herself from laughing out loud because her shoulders started to shake up and down. She very quickly regained composure and began to handle the situation. My mother was called, my father was called, and I just wanted to crawl under a rock because of the dilemma my crush had caused. Carl Lehman never even got reprimanded —only me. I was going "solo" on this deal and I did too, all the way through it. My mother was as cool as a cucumber in her attempts to downplay the incident. She started by telling Mrs. Sandoval, "Well you know, children are children, and I'm sure my child isn't the first person to do this type of thing." There was this very long, awkward pause, and when Mrs. Sandoval finally spoke, she looked my mother right in the eye and said, "Mrs. Hood, this *is* the first time this has ever happened at this school and so your child *is* the exception."

I would go back to class that day only to have to listen to the teacher berate me in front of the other students and continually blame me for every other thing that went wrong with her day. I couldn't wait for the year to end. I sensed that Mrs. Killibrew was herself emotionally driven and that my ticks and quirks and impulsivity only added fire to *her* condition. I did hear my father (later that night) telling Mrs. Killibrew (by phone) that she just needed to "kick some ass and take some names." I panicked, thinking "NO! Don't tell her that! That's the last advice she needs to hear because you have no idea what she does and says to me when you're not around."

My actions that morning concerning Carl and the window were less than admirable, but my actions never warranted the continual onslaughts I received after that incident. I think had my parents known of my teacher's behavior toward me, they would have had a much different conversation with Principal Sandoval. In the months following the incident, Mrs. Killibrew's own peers would stand in the hallway cringing as they listened to her berate me for minor things. My teacher would find everything under the sun wrong with me, and it noticeably bothered her coworkers.

The day after the bookcase incident, I was at recess and I found myself looking down from a small hill into a ballfield. I stood there and the thought hit me about the events of the day before. I thought to myself, "I'm different! I don't know why I'm different, but I'm different. And you know what? I think I like it!" I went back inside Mrs. Killibrew's classroom that afternoon and sat down, and for the first time all year I smiled inside. I had made myself look at my incident through a different set of lenses. Deep inside, I was starting to see that things were looking up.

The impulsivity caused by ADD or ADHD is something that people with the condition eventually outgrow. When their brain develops and their cognitive abilities mature, they gain more control and are not so compelled to be impulsive. Impulsivity is such a noticeable trait while the ADD/ADHD person is young only because cognitively they haven't had the opportunity to grow into higher-level thinking. I found that my impulsive behavior really decreased as I got older. I developed new coping skills and could apply those skills to circumvent my impulses. My life became much calmer as I became truly able to think things through, to weigh actions and consequences. Thank God! Impulsivity combined with hyperactivity can really be lethal to the child who doesn't know how to harness them early on.

Hyperactivity can also negatively affect the health of a person with ADHD later in life. I have exercised all my life because it calmed me down, but I especially made it a priority after I turned sixteen. I found exercise to be a release for the energy that would build up in my body due to hyperactivity. I also found that when I exercised good chemicals, endorphins, were released in my body that would make me feel really good. I have exercised to this day because I love the way it makes me feel. However, even with good exercise and eating right, I have had to get on blood pressure medicines. I believe my high blood pressure is due to the hyperactivity that comes with ADHD, but some might say it is just because of my genes. My father died at forty-six of an aneurysm. Whether my high blood pressure is caused by my ADHD or my genes, I have always tried to be an avid exerciser to deter this particular health issue.

Heart problems seem to run in my father's family, and many in his family have died at early ages. I noticed this pattern when I was younger, but now I see other patterns, particular traits, in his side of the family. I notice that all of those relatives who died early, including my father, were all ultrahyper. They always had to be busy and never knew how to rest and allow their bodies to just relax. I don't know whether that was just how their generation responded to life or if this hyperactivity was related to each individual's personality makeup.

I made up my mind to try to take good care of my body and eat right to keep hyperactivity to a minimum. I do notice when the energy build up happens (some might call it anxiety or stress), but I make sure to give that energy an outlet through exercise. I have also found that my blood pressure medicines help to maintain lower hyperactivity.

Chapter 2

My Struggles
in Education

I really didn't notice that I struggled in education until I was in high school. What I did notice was that I would excel in certain areas of study, while doing very poorly in others. What most astounded me was that I could be in one teacher's classroom and do very poorly in a subject and then go into a different teacher's class and ace that same subject. This particular phenomenon confused me. I didn't understand it, but I noticed the pattern.

I never really applied myself in school because when I tried it was like being in a huge ocean trying to figure out which direction to go. There were too many details. I would find out later that my brain was struggling to organize information so that I could process and then learn it. I was always too busy being distracted by daydreaming and looking out the window and thinking of when I would grow up. I was going to go to Paris or be in the movies or become someone famous. I was going to do BIG things . . . that was until Mrs. Johnson, my second grade math teacher, came over to me and said, "Melissa, if you don't stop that daydreaming, you're never going to get your times tables done." She then very gently took me to the back of the class and sat me down and started using visual cue cards. I learned my times tables so fast that day that it shocked both her and me! But I was happy and I liked Mrs. Johnson because she seemed to love us as students. She was this very kind black lady who you just wanted to hug because she was always such a loving person. She never seemed to pay attention to my quirks and ticks but instead just let me be me. I felt at home in her classroom. There was another little girl that was in her class with me whose name was Ilona (that's pronounced I—LONA). Ilona had Down syndrome and Mrs. Johnson would always sit her at my table. Ilona and I got along really well, and it didn't ever phase me that she looked different or had a disability. I sometimes wondered why her eyes looked slanted when mine didn't, but to me she was just another friend for me to play and learn alongside. Besides she was one of the few friends that accepted me. She just struggled a little bit in her speech, but with my hyperactivity always making me buzz around I hardly think I noticed. My gosh! My whirlwind world was always keeping me so busy that someone else's flaws were never something I could take notice of. I had enough of them myself.

Special Ed classes didn't exist for special needs kids back then. They didn't have separated classes thirty-five years ago. All the special needs kids were put into regular classrooms with the rest of the student population. This never bothered me much because my parents never made me feel that something was wrong with me, nor had I been diagnosed. The lack of separation also enabled me to think of and see other children with learning disabilities as being normal and just regular students. My condition would go unnoticed for the first few years until I got into high school, which required higher-level learning. What people did notice early on was that I drove everybody crazy with my hyperactivity.

The Mrs. Johnsons of the world made my life bearable. With her, and other teachers like her, I always felt safe. I knew that they would love me for me, and their love prepared me for all of the mean-spirited teachers I would later encounter who would misunderstand, reject, or verbally and emotionally abuse me because of my ADHD. When Mrs. Johnson would see me struggling, she would say, "Melissa, it's just water on a duck's back, let it roll off." This was easier to do when I was younger, but it got harder as I grew older and was trying to master more difficult subjects and encountering meaner people. The distractions became so great, and with my mind being all over the radar screen all the time, it was hard for me to concentrate. I found my distracted state only increased until I got older and acquired better coping skills for paying attention. These allowed me to focus and learn. Before then, everything distracted me, everything from the sun shining outside, to the birds chirping, to people tapping their pencils on their desks. It was like my brain picked up on every noise, every sight—and it was just awful.

I would later find out that ADHD kids are ultrasensitive to bright lights (mainly fluorescent), smells, and sounds. To this day I am easily frightened or shocked by sudden noises. My sensitivity to loud environments is very apparent. I find that if there is too much noise, I quickly become overstimulated, which makes me irritable. This irritability now signals me to find a quiet place where my brain can calm down and relax. This quiet allows me to focus and finish the task at hand. I also find that if I focus for too long on a topic my brain gets tired easily. So I have to take "brain breaks" and allow myself to do something else that's not so intense. After the break, I can maintain focus and stay on task. I work in twenty- to thirty-minute intervals when I'm trying to get a task done. If I don't take breaks, I also get really bad headaches and sometimes start to feel nauseated. I know it sounds strange, but it's the truth.

I also learned something else very important about myself and this wonderful "brain o' mine." I learned that I excel in subjects when teachers engage me in all four learning styles. I came to see the pattern after attaining my BA. I discovered I was not only an audial learner, but a visual, hands-on, and repetitious learner. Most students only need the audial portion to learn, but students with ADD/ADHD need all four styles at the same time.

Mrs. Johnson used several styles with me that day when she took me to the back of the class to do my times tables.

She held up cue cards (visual) and spoke the numbers—"two times two equals?" (audial)—and ran through the same cards several times (repetition). Using multiple styles, she held my interest; she fully engaged my brain. Mrs. Johnson would also give me the time I needed to process the information, which many teachers do not do with special needs students. When I had thought of the number, my brain became engaged like it was a game. I would see how fast I could remember the answers, which made the learning fun. The cards were being shown to me over and over so I learned the game very quickly. Repetition is systematic and it creates structure. Each of these learning styles has a part in creating the needed structure for the ADD/ADHD brain. If there is no structure, we feel like we're in an ocean of information. When I was younger, if you handed me a sheet of paper with information typed on it for me to read, and the text was on white paper with black ink, my brain would get completely overwhelmed. I didn't know how to distinguish the major points of information from the minor points. I would later learn to use colored highlighters to aid my brain in seeing and processing these distinctions.

My quick learning of numbers with Mrs. Johnson happened because she taught in a very systematic way. And math is a structured subject. Those of us with ADHD minds are naturally systematic thinkers. If our brain can put things in order, it can make sense out of the information. So any subject taught in a systematic or structured way (and taught with all four learning styles) engages our brains to activate, participate, learn, and . . . retain! We're in the game, we're engaged, and we're not bored.

My brain is always thinking of the best way to get from Point A to Point B in the least amount of time with the least amount of effort. I can usually look at any problem that I'm dealing with from five different perspectives at once. I am systematic in my approach so I look at circumstances differently, being able to filter out everything that's not important and being able to see the practical elements that make up the problem and the solution. When I was younger, all the distractions would hinder my brain from focusing on the elements most important to finding solutions. The prescription drug Adderall has been critical to the development of my cognitive skills, allowing my brain to mature and move into higher-level thinking and learning.

Most people get really impatient with me when I'm thinking over a problem because they aren't looking at the problem the way I do. They usually make a rush to judgment pressing me to make a decision, which can cause mistakes, resulting in more work having to be done all the way around. This would happen to me often when I was younger, and I ended up doing double the work, which I hated. This type of impatience irritates me, because if everyone will just give ADD/ADHD people the time they need to find the "right" solution, it can be a huge timesaver for all parties. I understand that some situations need instant answers, but I also know my ADHD can be a tremendous gift in finding solutions to problems with a lot of components. I see the big picture and am a visionary. It's part of the gift of ADHD. I can create good change and see that things get done right the first time, if I am allowed to use my gift. And yes! ADHD *is* a tremendous gift!

Having ADHD made making friends at school hard. My hyperactivity and impulsiveness either made others nervous or didn't allow them enough time to sit down and get to know me. Kids didn't understand me and so I was made fun of a lot. I had ticks, or quirks—like sniffling all the time—that other kids would either laugh at or just shake their heads. They thought it was strange. I used to try to get around this by saying "excuse me (sniffle), pardon me (sniffle), (cough) excuse me," but after a hundred times of hearing that, how could anybody not think I had a problem? I sniffled a great deal in ninth grade. My best friend and I had the same class, and she would laugh until she cried because she thought I was doing it deliberately to irritate our history teacher, Mrs. Smith. Mrs. Smith hated my sniffling and would tell me to "stop that nonsense" because it was disruptive, but I couldn't help it because it was a tick, and if I could have stopped I would have—believe me. Now when the tick comes on, I just sniffle and keep my mouth shut and don't explain myself. Let 'em all think I'm crazy. Oh well, what can you say?

Home was my safe place, and so I found myself staying very close to both my parents in an effort to be in an accepting environment. Ticks and quirks are funny things, but my parents never noticed them.

I had a hard time making eye contact with people because I was so hyper. It was like my brain couldn't keep my eyes on anyone long enough to hold a conversation. In my teen years, I found myself forcing myself to look someone in the eye for the duration of a conversation, which was almost unbearable at times because my brain was all over the place. To make things worse, the individual I was talking to usually started to feel a little uncomfortable with the intensity of my gaze and would even start fidgeting and trying to get out of the conversation. I found this tick technique to be very unsuccessful. The person I was talking to would either think I was weird or someone with a mental problem. I guess people felt I was staring at them too long. They didn't know that I was trying to overcome a tick. If I didn't force myself to maintain eye contact and focus, my head would have been bobbling all over the place to everything my brain was distracted to. This tick did get better as I got older, and I have taught myself the three-second rule: look someone in the eye for three seconds, and then look away; make eye contact again for three seconds, then look away. So far this technique has really helped my social skills. ("Thank God," most of you are probably saying!) Ticks and quirks, and my bluntness have made socializing hard at times, and so I hang out with friends that really love me for me and try not to worry about everything else.

Relating to people was a challenge, but I was more intimidated by learning because my teachers didn't know what to do. They didn't understand the way I learned. I might have seemed inattentive, but only because the learning style used was usually one-sided. It benefitted the teacher but not the student. I either didn't understand what they were teaching, or was bored because I had already worked through the problem and it was too easy. I can understand their frustration, too, because when I did learn, I learned very quickly, and when I couldn't, well, I just couldn't. It was like an on-off switch, and the lights were either on or nobody was home.

In fourth grade, I was in Mrs. Penndel's class (she was a super nice teacher), and though I liked her, I didn't totally get her teaching style. One day after the entire fourth grade took the California Achievement Tests, she pulled me aside and asked me how I did what I did. I was like "What? What did I do?" She told me that I had scored the highest in the entire school on my test. Yet I didn't do well in my classes. I believe this was in part because I wasn't grasping some subjects while I did grasp all or parts of others. This was due to teaching styles and my interest in those subjects as opposed to others.

I found this learning pattern repeated in high school and in college. I would excel in classes, no matter what the subject, when I had a teacher who could teach in all four learning styles. These teachers were also good communicators and didn't expect me (or any student) to read their minds. They understood the information that they were teaching, but knew that I didn't, and they could pinpoint the misunderstanding in my learning. Their teaching style wasn't just audial. These successful teachers used audial, visual, and repetitious techniques, and then allowed me to repeat back to them what I understood. They could then fill in the blanks of what I didn't understand. When taught this way, I could learn super quickly.

The ADHD brain has to be engaged on all levels to learn. People with ADD/ADHD are interactive with their environments, and when we can engage on multiple levels, we're teachable. I believe the problems I have encountered with learning are twofold. I have come to the conclusion that most teachers teach from their own preferred style of learning, but that style of learning might not suit all students. If the ADD/

ADHD brain isn't taught in all four learning styles, I believe it will respond just like mine did, grasping some subjects but not others, or at least not wholly, just in part.

For instance, in a history class, a teacher might deliver the information by taking me back in time through telling a story (audial) and then by showing slide presentations (visual). The teacher might even present the same material in a different way like in a game (repetition), or get me to stand up and talk about what I know on the subject. This is interactive learning. Field trips are also a great way to implement interactive learning and can be used to reinforce previously taught material. Whenever the ADD/ADHD mind is taught this way, it is fully engaged, both absorbing and retaining information because that information has been brought to life! We love to experience what we learn!

Have you ever heard people say that someone is a "late bloomer" in life? When this is said about me, I completely disagree. When I began taking ADHD meds (Adderall), they totally changed my life. What most people don't understand is that the medicine is what allowed my brain to fire consistently so that I could focus enough to learn higher-level critical thinking skills. The effect of the medication is what enabled my brain to mature emotionally and cognitively. The ADHD mind (without medicine) does not fire consistently, preventing progress in cognitive and emotional abilities. I feel the late-bloomer label is unfair. I would have "bloomed" just fine had my condition been diagnosed twenty-five to thirty-five years ago instead of just seventeen years ago. With a diagnosis and the aid of medicine, I would have progressed and advanced faster. I was always a very quick learner when I could focus and become engaged in what I was studying.

ADD/ADHD kids are very literal thinkers. We perceive life the way *we* see it. We tend to struggle when we get around those who aren't skilled communicators because we are so literal in our processing of information. We say what we mean and we mean what we say. This literalness can be a stumbling block, because not everyone has strong, clear communication styles.

Ever heard of the book *Amelia Bedelia*? Its main character, Amelia Bedelia, is very literal. If you commanded her to draw the drapes, Amelia would literally sit down with a pad of paper and pen and draw a picture of the drapes. You might have meant for her to pull your curtains back on each window, but because she is so literal, she does what she *perceives* you mean for her to do. I believe a lot of students misconstrue information and instructions given to them because of a lack of understanding about their need for clear communication. This is very common with ADD/ADHD people as I myself have experienced. I am not a mind reader, nor can I read between the lines to know what others are thinking when they are talking to me. I can't do that with teachers or bosses or anyone. I've had to learn and have taught myself to ask good questions of my teachers and bosses so that I can get the information needed to complete the tasks that they are requesting of me.

I also believe that many in society have forgotten how to communicate effectively. Nobody seems to say what they mean or mean what they say anymore, and hence, here we are with this huge communication problem. But that's another topic to be written about in another book perhaps.

"Literal thinking" is a part of my interaction with my environment. I say what I see—literally. This truthfulness, or bluntness, is a result of an ADD/ADHD person's thought process. We say what we see because we see the world with a childlike simplicity. This has become more problematic for me over the years because I found that people didn't like the bluntness of my conversations. My own immediate family didn't have any problems with this, but extended members sure did. They still do when they interact with me because people don't always want to know the literal truth and would rather skirt the real issues. Personally, I find that to be crap because when we relate there are going to be issues. If we don't allow ourselves or others to be honest, to be real, the issues won't get reconciled. You have to be able to deal with the truth in order to remove barriers, to resolve conflict. However, too much truth can be very hurtful, so you have to measure it out to the heart you are communicating with.

I have had to retrain myself (over time) to hold back in conversation and not just say exactly what's on my mind, because it offends people. My bluntness caused a lot of problems in my workplace until I learned stronger social skills regarding disclosing information. I have learned that not everyone can handle deep truths about a person or their circumstances until they have gravitated into deeper levels of relating with them. This occurs during the normal progression of relationships. Those of us with ADD/ADHD have a hard time remembering that our actions bring consequences, and so we struggle with understanding the progression of relationships. Bottom line: You don't disclose your most private information to a perfect stranger, and the same applies to a person you are trying to connect with to form a new relationship. "TMI" (too much information) overwhelms people, and until they know your heart, they probably can't accept the true you. I think of this as not throwing your pearls before swine. Not everybody in this life has the best of intentions toward you; therefore, not everybody deserves to see the deepest part of your heart.

Taking my time getting to know others was just using wisdom, but I had to retrain my brain to do it. Today, in my relationships, I hold back until I see the other person's heart and their intentions toward me. Only when I see that their heart is safe to relate with do I move into deeper levels of a relationship. This caution keeps me from walking around wounded. Believe it or not, this is how you formulate really meaningful relationships—romantic or not. It is a process, and one not to be taken lightly. You should consider yourself "precious cargo"—especially your heart. This was very hard for me for many years and caused big problems in all my relationships growing up. I started working on my relationship skills about thirteen years ago and have made tremendous headway as I made needed changes.

In all honesty, I love it when people are blunt and truthful with me because this is the way that I deal with my world and with others that know me. I have just had to learn to speak the truth in love and how to measure certain amounts of information out while relating. The truth spoken literally can be very hurtful to a heart that's not geared to relate the same way as I am.

People with ADD/ADHD, whether kids or adults, see their world through the level of maturity that they are at emotionally, and we will relate with others at that level as well.

A lack of emotional maturity presents a special problem for those of us struggling with the ADD/ADHD. People often cross our paths posing as "Good Samaritans." These Good Samaritans appear to be trying to help us establish order when in reality they are predators who prey on those they deem weak or easily manipulated. They are abusers and users, both verbally and emotionally, and sometimes physically, and they see us as people to be disrespected—until we figure them, and their motives, out.

This type of abuse happened to me over and over again until I was able to recognize the type. The Good Samaritan would come into my life and start off treating me well, but then the verbal and emotional abuse would subtly start. Early on, in my immaturity, I trusted these people and would let them just come on into my life. As a consequence, I found myself walking wounded all the time because so often people wanted to manipulate or control me for their own screwed-up purposes. They did this by trying to smother or dominate my time, by controlling me with their rage issues, by using false guilt on me, by verbal criticalness, or withholding love ("If you let me control you, then I will accept and love you"). These behaviors are clearly emotional abuse and happened to me over and over in jobs, even within my church, until I got more whole. I found that when I began to heal and develop more in my cognitive abilities, I could discern their motives. I became able to recognize them (both in my family and in the outside world) and avoid their dysfunction. Quick clue: healing starts from within not from without, so controlling others or being controlled by them is not going to bring healing to you as an individual. When people control others, they are attempting to gain control over the chaos in their own worlds. The only person allowed to control me is God.

Those of us with ADD/ADHD have enough chaos without these nuts adding to it. I didn't know that I had an undiagnosed condition, but when controlling people saw my life, they believed I was in need of their help to bring it under control. No thanks! I don't want that brand of love. I didn't need them controlling me—I just needed to be diagnosed so that I could learn and advance like any other human being. I would give this advice to people without ADD/ADHD too—to me, it is just good mental health.

At thirty-five, a lot of the chaos in my life diminished because I was able to focus on my relationship skills and finally progress and draw healthier people into my sphere, people who really know what loving relationships are and how loving people behave.

People that love you protect you; they look out for you and hold you accountable. Loving people don't try to make decisions for you, they respect your boundaries and understand that NO means NO. Period. End of story. I don't want to fix anybody and I don't want to be fixed—I just want people around me to love and accept me for who I am. It's all I've ever wanted. In this, I am just like any other human being, with ADHD or without. I want to be loved flaws and all—but in a healthy way.

Discernment is key. Our lives will stay in chaos if we don't learn to set healthy boundaries and standards with those around us. Unhealthy people are drawn to those of us with ADD/ADHD. I believe the rejection that many of us have experienced from not knowing what was wrong with us makes us vulnerable. NOTHING is wrong with you! You just learn differently! Did you know that you are (I'm ultraserious about what I'm getting ready to say) a borderline if not a full-fledged genius because of your abilities and the way that you perceive the world and learn???!!!

So for those who have not yet been able to come into a place of order—you sometimes have to create that order by making yourself find new playmates and new playgrounds. When you send people who have been causing you problems away from you, you might go through a short season of loneliness, but that's bound to change as you change and get whole! Remember: You draw those to yourself who are like you, and as your life comes into order so will your relationships! You can never control others, and others NEVER have the right to control you because of your disability. You are not a victim, but you can be victimized by other's perception of the disorder in your life if you let those types of personalities into your life.

YES!!!!! I'm an OVERCOMER and SO ARE YOU!

Chapter 3

TEENAGE YEARS
Drill Team Bullying

My high school years were not too bad at the start. I quickly learned that the way to be accepted was to be in social activities. My mother had me take dance lessons—tap, jazz, ballet, and twirling—for eight years of my life to help keep my weight down, so trying out for the high school drill team was a way to both dance and be accepted—the best of two worlds. My past dance experience helped me to make the team, but that also opened me up to another set of problems.

Our drill team was renowned for national competitions and being the best in the state, but even that status didn't guarantee acceptance for me. My experiences on the team would provoke my ADHD condition and would also show me a very different and evil side to people.

ADHD's number one trigger is stress, and the stress of having to maintain a 75 average and then learn all the choreography for Friday night games proved to be too much for me. I still didn't have strong enough coping skills, and teachers still didn't teach in all learning styles. I found myself not doing well in a lot of my classes. I was put on academic probation twice, and after the second time, I was kicked off the team eight months into the year.

Throughout the entire eight months, I had noticed the drill team instructor's hidden vitriol toward me. Her dislike became openly apparent after I went to my history teacher and requested extra homework credit. I requested the homework to raise my GPA to the needed 75% required to stay on drill team. To me, it always seemed that I had to do double what the average student did to participate in extracurricular activities. This added effort created more stress on top of the stress that always accompanied learning. So unbeknownst to myself, I was basically experiencing triple the average student's stress—from academic learning, drill team learning, and then having to worry about my average and seek out extra assignments to keep my GPA up. Crazy.

I loved history and so I had gone to my history teacher and requested to read five extra books in order to meet the 75 GPA standard. My teacher agreed to this. The effort did pay off, raising my GPA to above the 75 GPA. But this extra credit was not good enough for Mrs. Miller, the drill team instructor. She notified me that she was still going to stand behind her original decision to force me off the team.

My father went to her office to dispute her decision. He told her that her actions were wrong and unjust. He told her that I had indeed met her requirements and had brought my GPA up, and then he questioned if her actions were prompted by something else. I knew that my dad saw that I struggled in my academics, but he was willing to fight for me because he also knew I had done the work. I might never know what Mrs. Miller's actions were really prompted by except to say that I had sensed that she thought I didn't try hard enough to learn the routines. Had she asked me, she might have found out that I was struggling in my learning all the way around.

My mother and I have talked about this over the years, and we have both settled on one truth. We both agree that the stress caused by having to maintain a certain GPA coupled with the constant stress of learning new routines (which ADHD people don't do well) hindered my ability to perform. Honestly though, inside my heart, I always sensed that my presence on the drill team was met with bigotry, hypocrisy, and malice. I felt that I was barely tolerated. I was always treated badly by the instructor, and the girls she led, because of her own lack of knowledge about me. It seemed so important to these other girls to have the drill team instructor's approval that they emulated her own bad behavior toward me. I was intensely bullied.

The bullying consisted of behaviors such as hiding parts of my uniform, which I would get reprimanded for not having, and making snide and critical remarks to belittle me in front of others while we were in practice. Mrs. Miller was harder on me than on the other girls. I remember when a senior and I both had our hair cut short during the competition season. Mrs. Miller reprimanded me for getting mine cut but praised the other girl. This is just a small sample of the bullying I experienced.

Today, I would have had grounds for a lawsuit against these people for severe harassment. Their behaviors got so bad at one point that one of the seniors took a stand for me one day in practice. I've never forgotten her words to Mrs. Miller. Olivia Casey was bold and loving enough to stick up for me publically. She told Mrs. Miller and the girls that their behaviors toward me were inexcusable and extremely abusive. Mrs. Miller's only response was "Yes, Missy has come a long way, and we need to treat her better." The comment dismissed her own bad behavior and shifted everyone's attention off the truth and onto something that made her feel more comfortable, my inadequacies.

That was the day that my eyes were opened to behaviors that had gone on toward me all my life in many other circumstances. I had taught myself to overlook them, but the pain had buried itself deep. I guess I had stuffed it down and tried to focus on other things that were going well in my life. This particular incident changed me. For the first time, I understood how evil people could be toward those they deemed different.

I was very grateful to my dad for taking a stand and calling this woman out on her injustices toward me. He knew I loved him, and he was always a truth seeker, standing up for others who needed protection. My parents have been my strongest allies. Although I was different, they saw something in me that I hadn't seen in myself yet.

In my heart back then, even though I knew I didn't learn like the other students and knew I was different, I didn't see this as something necessarily bad. I did see it as a pain in the butt because I knew I wasn't stupid. Things would have turned out so differently had I known then what I know now. But I guess it's the mountains we climb in this life that make or break us, and I have NO regret about having climbed this particular one!

I missed out on getting my letter jacket that year. To most of you reading this, that probably does not sound like a big deal, but it sure was to a sixteen year old who had worked to the best of her abilities.

Mrs. Miller was also a neighbor of ours, and she continued to be for twenty years after that incident. Talk about hard! After that year, I completely lost respect for her. She would drive by my house and wave, and all I could do was turn and walk the other way. I couldn't even look at her because all I saw was a woman who really didn't care about me, a woman who only cared for herself and her reputation and about appearing successful to others. God help anyone who ever made her look otherwise. She never sat me down during that season and asked me what I was struggling with or tried to find ways to assist me with my studies. Instead she judged and humiliated me and used the immaturity of other girls to bully me into submission.

Some ten years later, I did speak my mind to Ms. Miller. I was in an undergrad program and was trying to be awarded college credits for some of my high school experience so that I could graduate early. I needed her to fill out some forms for a particular class, verifying the experience in dance that I gained on the drill team in high school. I had felt some reluctance about approaching her, but the credits would save me time and money so I decided to ask her. I did get awarded eighteen college credit hours through CLEP, the College Level Exam Program, along with taking sixteen credit hours in courses that semester. I thought I was going to have a nervous breakdown with the college workload, but I also found out that I wasn't stupid. The professors at St. Edwards University made it possible for me to succeed. Because I was in a smaller university, I was able to have a lot of one-on-one time with each of my professors, and they all went above and beyond to help me! I was so grateful.

But back to Mrs. Miller. True to form, she somehow had lost the forms I had placed on her side porch (where she asked me to put them). She then had the audacity to stop by my house on Christmas Eve, just as my mother and I were about to leave for church, to chide me about "my negligence."

My mother and I were just getting into my vehicle when she drove up and rolled down her window. She started reprimanding me, "Missy, why didn't you put those forms on my porch?!!" She made it sound like she actually had a right to be angry. This was the same way she used to accuse me when I was on the high school drill team. But this time, things were different. I was a little more mature, hopefully wiser, and my eyes were opened as opposed to times past.

Her words triggered a lot of anger in my heart. I was so angry at her after all the abuse I had taken on drill team that I was loaded for bear! Inside I thought: "She's got a lot of gall to stand there and turn the truth around like I've done something wrong. She acted like she was doing me some big favor in the first place or like I had put her out for even asking, good god!"

My response to her was curt and blunt. I looked her right in the eye and said: "I *did* put the forms on your side porch, ma'am—I put them in an envelope where you asked me to put them. I even put a rock on them to hold them down to ensure that you would see them. You couldn't have missed them. Obviously, you did overlook them just like you have dismissed everything I have tried to accomplish since I've known you. *You* dropped the ball on this one, not me."

Her response was stunning: "Missy, are you saying that I didn't want to help you, because I did." She probably did misplace the forms, or the wind blew them away, but somehow in my heart I just couldn't believe anything she had to say to me anymore. She had lost my respect and confidence twelve years earlier. It's amazing to me when those who wrong you forget their actions have consequences—or is that just for their convenience?

My final response to her was this: "Yes—that's exactly what I'm saying. But don't worry yourself, Mrs. Miller, really, because I found the information that I needed, and I ended up CLEPing out of eighteen hours on my own, without your help. So, thanks and have a Merry Christmas!"

I had the vindication I had waited twelve years for that night! Mrs. Miller had always known me to be very honest and forthright. I didn't lie and I did what I told people I would do because that was the way I was raised. I cannot help that my disability hindered my efforts to learn way back then. I've forgiven her, but I won't ever tolerate those behaviors from anyone again. Her emotional abuse coupled with the bullying by all the other girls had really done a number on my self-esteem.

What I do know in my heart of hearts is that my father taught me that I could do anything that I set my heart to despite the ignorance or unkindness of other people. He taught me that there were always going to be ignorant people who would try to beat me down for what they didn't understand.

I will always be a woman of my word, and I ask you to mark these: I will NOT be held back any longer by abusers or bullies because I'm in the know now, and so are you. My experience with Mrs. Miller would prepare me for the many times after that Christmas Eve when I would have to take a stand against abusive people. I had never stood up for myself before, but that time I did, and it was huge and brought much healing.

Chapter 4

MY TWENTIES
I Hate Changes—The Chaos in My Life

"Say it isn't so, Joe!" I finally turned twenty, I was dating my second boyfriend, and I was noticing that things were not going so well. I didn't have the same problem with my first boyfriend because he loved me unconditionally, and so this second relationship would end up being an eye-opening experience. It was the first time that I noticed that my ticks and quirks were getting on somebody else's nerves.

Kyle and I had been dating for two years. I was still reeling from the self-esteem problems that high school had created. I felt like I was struggling with so many things but couldn't pinpoint any one of them particularly, except to say that I was very unhappy in my life. I guess maybe I felt like I had failed. I felt I had given into the fear that had kept me from going to college. I had been intimidated by the idea. My fear of failing was so huge that I figured—Why try? I'll fail out anyway. I had barely passed high school, and the thought of putting myself through that all over again was a little more than I could bear. My grades were OK in high school. It was the stress behind the learning that most intimidated me.

I distinctly remember my mom and dad saying "Missy, if you don't go to college, it will be harder for you to advance in life, and we don't want you to have to struggle like we did." The problem was that I was already struggling and having a hard time coping with a condition that I didn't even know I had. I knew something was wrong, but my way of dealing with it was just to look on the brighter side of life and do what I thought I could do well. I was starting to drink too much because I couldn't cope with the truth that something might be wrong. Being numb was better than always being depressed. Was I just stupid or was the problem that I just didn't want to listen to others trying to push me down a path that I knew I would fail in? My father pressured me so much and kept offering to pay my tuition every time I turned around if I would just "try" to go to school. I finally broke and said "OK!" To make him leave me alone, I would attempt college a second time only to find out that I was right, and it turned out just like I knew it would. I would go to class and the classes were so fast paced that I couldn't keep up with the reading and focusing, so to me it was all just pointless.

An individual with an undiagnosed ADHD condition is about as successful in college as a whale outside of water. I was floundering in my attempts and everyone saw it. I didn't have the medications that would have helped me to focus so that I could take notes and retain information. At this point, my whole world was out of control. I had graduated from a structured environment (high school) and was now in college, where I had to create my own structure. I was doubly lost: I didn't know I needed structure to help me in my learning, and I didn't know how to create it. I did still have my dad's military structure. He made schedules and issued deadline reminders; however, he was trying to let go of the reins, thinking he was helping me to mature. I later found out that the structure he provided was the only support I had to do what they wanted me to do. A lot of people would have said I was immature and not ready to go back to school; however, I would disagree. Deep inside I longed to be like everyone else and learn quickly and gain an education. Nobody ever knew about all the times that I would drive down by UT (University of Texas) and secretly wish that I could perform at the level of other students, that I could be successful in school. No one knew why I cut my classes or what I experienced when I tried to sit and learn. I was so frustrated, and the anger was becoming very apparent to everyone around me. My inability to learn made me feel like a complete loser. I just felt so defeated inside.

My brother, on the other hand, seemed to have no problems learning. He was in college and doing very well and working on his architectural career. He had always been studious and intelligent, and academics always seemed to come easily for him.

I began partying. It was the one thing I was good at and so I focused on that. My mother and father saw I was starting to spiral out of control. My staying out all night and my partying were creating friction between us. They saw me moving into a fast lane lifestyle that they knew they hadn't raised me to live in. My boyfriend was involved in extracurricular activities that I disagreed with, and so his behavior was quickly becoming a hot topic within our relationship. I was ashamed and confused, but I still knew in my heart that God had put a dream there. My only problem was that I didn't know how to get to where I wanted to be because of this one stupid obstacle: LEARNING!

This confusion would go on in my life until my twenty-second year when my entire world would turn upside down in the blink of an eye. October 31, 1987 would be the day that my life would be changed forever.

Every year my family would get together to go and cut wood for the winter. It was a major event that everybody participated in. This year, the day started very differently because I had been out all night the night before and was hungover. I knew that my father was going to expect me to get up and go with them on this outing because it was something we always did. My father had been my rock, but lately he and I hadn't been on such good terms because like any young adult I thought I knew everything. He, however, saw through this and knew I was struggling with something but didn't know how to help me. His unspoken concern was my constant reminder that someone was "on to me." The problem with me at this point in my life was that I had always thought that everything would work itself out. Any wisdom my dad had imparted fell on deaf ears. I was being driven by my own pain and undiagnosed ADHD. I felt like I had failed miserably, and the fact that I had failed him so badly was showing, so why should this particular day be unlike any other?

He came into my bedroom that morning and kissed me on my forehead and said, "Missy, it's OK if you don't want to go. I'll see you when I get home." His kiss would be the last one I would ever get from him, and it was the last time I would get to hug him ever again. I found the entire conversation strange; I knew something was different. I needed him to see success in my life, but I didn't know how to achieve it. I absolutely hated my life at this point because of all the pain I had gone through, the failures, the heartaches in relationships, everything just seemed to be getting more chaotic.

That day, October 31, at 10:25 a.m., my father would go down in a field cutting wood and die instantly of an aneurysm. I would hear the doorbell ring later that morning and find my brother's father-in-law and mother-in-law. They had come to take me to Lampasas, Texas. They had come to get me because my father had had a massive heart attack and the aneurysm. My worst nightmare had now come true—I had lost my rock.

So many people on my father's side of the family had died early in their forties because of heart disease, but I had always thought that my family was different or that we would beat it. Death couldn't happen to my family. My family wasn't like other families in that we loved each other deeply. My father was my best friend. I had lunch with him every Wednesday, faithfully, and then with my mother and him every Friday. I was very close to them even through my chaos. They were (my mom still is) my rocks that I had come to depend on for acceptance and security. I knew that they would always love me through thick and thin and that my failures, ticks, quirks didn't matter to them. They just saw me as "Missy" their youngest daughter, and I knew that I didn't have to perform for their love because their love was unconditional. It still is.

(This part was super painful for me to write so I decided to take a break.)

Sometimes in life there are just some things that absolutely matter, and unconditional love matters to a heart that seems different from others. I know I'm different, and I know God made me unique, but sometimes a heart has to wonder if God knew all the pain the differences would cause.

The day my dad died would turn my world upside down because nobody else around me knew how to engage me in my ADHD world. It is a tremendous blessing to be "known" by somebody by the spirit. To be known by the spirit by another human being means that that person understands you, accepts and loves you, flaws and all. They can understand how you tick, and they know how to help you to move through the seasons of your life. This is also what mentors do. But I had none. I was now in a terrible place, a huge ocean of heartache, and I was completely lost.

Chapter 5

HEAVENLY ENCOUNTERS
My Walk in Heaven

My dad's death would send me into a very hard place emotionally. I was not only dealing with an undiagnosed condition, I was dealing with major grief, and my only solution was to party more. I was totally out of control for that next year. I couldn't have cared less if I lived or died. I behaved like it too, and my friends were growing very concerned for my well-being.

It was in that next year, when I was twenty-three, that I had a heavenly encounter that sparked my outrage at God. In this encounter, I confronted Him over my losses, and this would lead me back to my roots.

I was lying in my bed one night after having been so depressed about everything in my life and my loss, and as I was lying there, I began to see what looked like an arch of white light. I started to see myself walk forward, but at the same time, I knew I was in bed. I heard a voice tell me "It's OK, come on in, you're on safe ground." I walked through the light into an open courtyard, and then I knew I wasn't in my bedroom anymore. The first thing I remember seeing was a beautiful cobblestone wall. It was stunning. I had never seen anything so magnificent. My senses were on overload. Everything around me was at the height of its splendor and just breathtakingly beautiful. I knew where I was, but I didn't, as I had never had an experience like this before in my entire life. I saw this gorgeous grassy knoll behind the wall with a pretty oak tree in it, and then I looked over to my left only to see this black man hoeing in a garden. He never looked up, he just kept hoeing in his garden. All of his vegetables were perfectly rounded, perfectly colored. Then I looked over to my right. Standing there was my father in a white robe, and I found myself instantly sprinting over to hug him. I bear-hugged him for real, and I never wanted to let go. I could feel his skin, and the warmth of his love for me was so strong, and I felt like I never wanted to leave this place where we were standing and hugging. He gently pulled back from the embrace, and I was surprised when I saw he was handing me a card. I got kind of confused, and I asked him if I was supposed to stay there with him, to which he responded "No Missy, you haven't accomplished what you set out to accomplish yet." I looked down at the card and it said "To Momma and Shawn" (my mother and brother). I opened it up. It said "I'm OK." I looked back over at the black man, and he was smiling at me. The next thing I knew I was back in my bed. I was in complete awe!

I got up that morning with a new vigor and more joy than I had ever felt in my entire life. I ran into my mom's bedroom and told her of my experience. We laughed and talked, and she agreed I had indeed walked in heaven and seen my dad.

The entire experience would change my life forever because from that point on the reality also hit me that if there was a heaven then there must also be a hell. I knew I had to tell everybody and warn them that heaven was REAL! Therefore, I needed to get to know this Jesus better, and so I went back to church and started dealing with my rage and frustration so that I could better understand what my dad had told me in heaven. I had experienced a miracle in that moment, but not the one God was fixing to grant me in helping me overcome this ADHD condition.

We all experience miracles every single day of our lives. I think we take so much for granted that we forget that God is the author and finisher of every single detail of our lives. I found out that He really did care about me, and that this crazy condition that I had suffered with all my life was about to change. Slowly but surely, He would begin to teach me things that only God could show a soul. The most precious thing He taught me, occurred when I began writing this book. I thought God was just trying to help me, but then I realized that God was in the miracle working business for many people not just me.

Ever heard of Temple Grandin? Temple Grandin was a child prodigy born with autism. She was and still is like an Einstein in her abilities to create inventions. She struggled with intimacy throughout her childhood years and up into college. She found solace in visiting her aunt and uncle's ranch in California. Her uncle worked with cattle, and she discovered that when she would get anxious if she could get into the cattle herder (it was this contraption that hugged each cow as it went through it or held it in place for branding), the hugging of the contraption would comfort her.

She would go on to invent gate openers for the ranch gates and later a cattle sorter that assisted at cattle auctions in maintaining and organizing the cattle that were being driven through the stables. She was and is an amazing human being! (Rent the movie with Claire Danes; it's called *Temple Grandin*.) My point in telling about Grandin is that sometimes our biggest "perceived" weaknesses will turn out to be our biggest strengths!

You know what? It's OK not to be OK with the way society says we have to be in order to be successful in this life! At forty-six, I'm finally coming to a place where I accept this condition myself, and you should too.

For many years though, really until I was thirty-seven, I was super insecure and unsure of everything about me. I would be diagnosed with ADHD when I was twenty-nine and just finishing college. Everybody thought I was crazy or had a mental illness, and my life was a mess! I was dating a man who was extremely abusive as was his family. In my family, I had never experienced this. No one ever would just land verbal onslaughts on a person for doing nothing. We weren't ever allowed to be unloving in my family. The situation with my boyfriend and his family showed me that I kind of lived in a bubble with the protection and love I had been surrounded by. I was raised in a family that was (and is) very close and loving to one another. We have our issues and we may not be perfect to each other or in agreement all the time, but we love, and love prevails. We may love each other from a distance at times too, but we LOVE.

Relationships are usually a struggle for people with ADD/ ADHD, or so the books say. You know what though? I only believe that to be true to a certain point. I don't believe it completely because I believe that love is the most powerful force on earth. I love, therefore, I can relate. I might not have done it so well when this condition was undiagnosed. Since then, I have grown and matured and so have my cognitive and emotional abilities. Medicine has helped me to focus, and seeking deep inner healing over the hurts from the past has also been essential. Through these two tools and the coping skills I have developed, I have learned to relate very effectively. I get kind of distant from people sometimes when they act crazy, and I may get very quiet when I disagree, but I know how to love. Love is a universal language and one every human being understands and reciprocates. Honestly, I found the majority of my healing in church, with the aid of a loving God named Jesus. I have gone through so much deep inner healing. Against all the odds, I have defied the stigmas that the world has tried to place on me. No force is more powerful than the love of Christ, and no man has the power to hold back His love for us when we allow Him to heal us. We may live in a world that seems to be giving up on Christ, but He never gives up on us.

He helped me to get out of a very abusive relationship with a man that didn't know the love of Christ any more than the man in the moon. Christ has helped me to overcome ADHD so that I can learn and progress just like any other student. Sometimes there are a few kinks, but nothing like before! I have been taking Adderall for fifteen years now, and it works very well for me. This is the best part though: I have finally received so much inner healing of my thinking (a battle of the mind over stress, the number one trigger of ADD/ADHD), that I only need to take my meds now about once every two to five months. Seriously! I have learned to apply coping skills, when under stress, and I know how to put those skills into place when I'm in learning environments. I can progress just like other students, and I learn just as fast if not faster. Don't tell me I don't serve an awesome God. Praise God! I will stake my life on this truth!

You see God takes the weak things of this world and uses them to confound the wise. He lifts up the "unlovelies" in this life to show the rest of the world who is God and who is NOT.

So now you know my secret, my secret tool in dealing with this condition. My life truly has become that of a walking talking miracle. My family has seen the changes and the healing that God has accomplished in me. God uses me to walk alongside of people like myself so that they too might receive that needed deep emotional healing and freedom from ADHD. I believe that inner healing is a major part of dealing with this condition because of the trauma we experience. This trauma fractures the mind spiritually. A mind that is fractured is like a piece of splintered wood in that it does not have a single eye (single focus), and therefore it cannot perform at its optimal ability. Deep hurts cause this splintering. I myself have walked through many types of abuse: sexual (from someone outside my family), verbal, emotional, and physical abuse (from a past boyfriend).

Taking Adderall, getting the needed inner healing, and then applying coping skills, all contribute to bringing people with ADD/ADHD to the true them inside, or "the single eye of faith." The single eye of faith occurs when your mind, will, and emotions are healed, like a broken vessel brought to wholeness, and you can progress in life.

I acquired this healing through two ministries: Chuck Pierce Ministries and Mark Chironna Ministries because God truly is in their midst when I listen. I listen online every Tuesday and Sunday. (Chuck Pierce Ministries has replays so I can work watching around my school schedule.)

I know that the science world would probably frown upon my conversation with many of you right now. I also know the name of Jesus scares a lot of folks because the mere mention of His name means change—change that occurs in a very different way, or in a way that might make you feel uncomfortable. I know that I have been let down by church people who didn't represent my savior in His truest form (love). But I also know that just having coping skills and taking medicine weren't the only things that healed my mind, nor could I have come this far with this condition using just those worldly tools. I needed something supernatural like Christ's healing and the two church ministries to help deal with the rejection and the traumas of the past. Supernatural doesn't include the occult, which is NOT of God or Jesus.

A lot of people in the world are seeking out answers through the supernatural, but not all things supernatural are good, pure, and lovely. The Bible says that if anything is good, pure, and lovely, think on these things. If things are evil or have an "aire" of darkness around them, they are not of God. The Bible also says that the enemy comes in like an angel or impure light. This particular type of light does have power—but it is not more powerful than Jesus' or God's power or light. The Bible clearly says that "greater is he that is in me than he that is in the world" (i.e. the devil and his seekers of false light, or false power). Everyone wants to be empowered these days, but if you are empowered by the wrong kind of light, then in essence, you really have no power. I don't know about you, but if I'm going to have to spend my life learning and warring against spiritual things, I want to make sure that I'm equipped with the right type of light and the right power—that which overcomes and dispels all darkness! Amen? Amen! You need the right tools to help dispel the darkness that is attacking your ability to think and process correctly! All of these tools combined allowed my brain to focus and function so that I could heal and learn and become who I am today.

God made me this way not so that I would feel imperfect, frustrated, or like I was just too broken to function normally. He wanted me to be able to come to Him just as I was (flaws and all) to show me His healing power. He's not a crutch; He's my friend and one of the most loving, kind friends I've ever known. I'm not ashamed to call Him friend in front of anybody. His love really has changed my life, and for those of you who would like to know Him, just say this simple prayer as I'm in agreement with you:

> *Father—please forgive me of my sins—Lord, I need help and I don't know how to deal with this condition or the hurts of my past by myself. The meds aren't enough and neither are the tools that I've tried to implement thus far. Please heal my mind and my heart, please come into my life, along with your Holy Spirit, and help me to become the person I was predestined to become.*
>
> *In Jesus' name, Amen.*

My heart really goes out to those who struggle with ADD/ADHD. I have experienced the pitfalls and the rejection from people I never thought I would experience it from. To those of you who are struggling or those who have struggled with some of the issues I've mentioned, I want you to know that you are not alone. I would so love to find you and, if you would allow me, I would hug you tightly to let you know everything was going to be alright. Things are going to be alright in your life, and if you choose, you can have success. The one thing that is important for your success is realizing that you can't do it all by yourself. There are a few choices that you will have to make, with God's help, so that you can have the future you dream of.

You are going to have to choose to develop stronger coping skills. If you are not on medicine, you need to consider using it in order to assist your brain function. Sometimes we need a little extra help and that's OK because needing help doesn't make you weak; it means you're a strong person for being able to ask. Do you believe that Christ can heal you? This is another topic that you might want to pray about because I know He can, but I had to choose to come to Him so that He could show me His power.

These are the first stepping stones to end your current frustration. God promises to be our ever-present help in time of need, and He's gone above and beyond to prove that to me over the years.

Let me tell you what Christ has done for me (in combination with new coping tools and meds):

I am now in graduate-level studies at Texas State University, standing where according to all the statistics I'm not supposed to be standing. The numbers all say (I hesitate to tell any ADD/ADHD student this) that out of all the students diagnosed with ADD/ADHD only 12% graduate from high school. The remainder go on to work in fast food, contractor, and construction jobs because they can't grasp higher-level learning. Out of that 12% only 7%–8% go on to attain their BA. Out of that 7%–8%, less than 4% will ever go on to MA or PhD programs (Kaminski, Turnock, Rosen, & Laster, 2006, pp. 60–61).

It is my goal to raise those numbers so that all students diagnosed with disabilities can go on to higher-level education to be able to achieve the dreams that God has placed into their hearts.

The stigmas that accompany these conditions are just that—stigmas. I want to educate students, universities, and society that these stigmas are not fair or accurate.

As students and human beings, we are not just "special needs" kids or people with a disability. We are walking, talking human beings with dreams and goals and the desire to advance and to achieve just like those who do not struggle with the condition. I refuse to allow anybody to label me or be a predictor of my future because only one person knows my future and that person also knows the number of my days.

Jesus said, "For I know the plans that I have for you, plans to prosper and not to harm you, but plans to give you hope and a future." I've read that scripture many times during my life. I've read it during some of my most challenging moments. I read it after I had been fired from a job because I couldn't grasp the material as fast as they would have liked. I read it after receiving a failing grade in a class that I had taken for the second time when I was younger. Deep within my heart, through all of these challenges, I knew that God could not lie. I knew He loved me and that He was working out all of this mess that I had walked through for my good. That's another promise in His word. He promises to work all things for the good for those who are in Christ Jesus. I know people don't like to talk about the supernatural or the things of the spirit and what the spirit of God can really do for us. But I do! I've read the Bible for years, from the time I was a little girl, and I made up my mind a long time ago in Lampasas, Texas, (when I saw His picture up on the wall) that I wanted to see with my own eyes the miracles of God. I wanted to see the Bible come to life right in front of me in my everyday environment and to see the captives set free. I wanted to see if it was real! And it is!!! His love is what life is all about. Love in abundance, to the fullest, until it overflows!

So to all those who have lived with this condition and struggled and made it this far, to where you're reading this book and looking for answers, keep reading! I applaud you and say: "Here! Here!" and "May God bless you!" I applaud you for having the courage and the endurance to run your race and not quit thus far!

For those of you with ADD/ADHD who have made it through to higher-level learning and even some who may be in honors programs, I also applaud you and challenge you to get out and come up alongside of another person struggling with the condition. None of us ever make it through this life without the help of another. It's what life is all about. We all need a little help from each other, and we need to learn and know that we can lean on each other for support with the hard things in life.

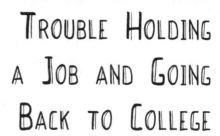

Chapter 6

Trouble Holding a Job and Going Back to College

I never really noticed any problems with my employment when I was young, but that was only because I was working in lower-level jobs that didn't require critical thinking skills. I seemed to always find myself working in fast food places in high school, and afterward in receptionist positions.

Eventually, I got tired of being in positions where I couldn't advance or in jobs that didn't challenge me. I wasn't in college yet, wasn't sure at this point that I wanted to go there, but found myself after the death of my father having to go there.

The stress seemed "gi-normous," but after a meeting with my mother and brother one Sunday afternoon, I became convinced that I needed to have a way to take care of myself. I would come to see that I needed to try going to college one more time—my third time.

I was afraid of this challenge. My biggest fear had already come to pass—the fear of losing my dad. He had been the one person who looked out for me with my ADHD challenges. He never made me feel like a victim but instead served as my encourager, someone I could depend on to motivate and make me believe. His Barnabas (encouragement) gifting made me believe that I really could do anything I set my heart and mind to. This time I just wasn't sure if I could do it alone. High school was hard enough, but college posed a completely different set of learning challenges that I was unsure I could master. I had tried twice before and failed miserably, and here I was up against this wall again.

So! I don't know how I did it, but I sucked up the fear, and somehow I got myself enrolled at ACC (Austin Community College). The pressure felt like a huge block on my shoulders, but I started to face the next biggest challenge of my journey by facing the fear that I had in my life of failing.

This time around, though, something was different. There was a new drive within me. I told myself that this time there were going to be self-imposed rules to push me forward.

The rules were

1. I couldn't quit, and
2. I couldn't take to heart any type of defeat or anything that would make me to want to quit.

It was a simple as that.

I had made up my mind this time that I would finish, no matter how hard it got, no matter what obstacle came before me. I was slowly starting to think differently, and my ability to process information (with the stopping and starting) was slowly beginning to change. I still wouldn't find out that I had a disability until four years later when I was twenty-nine. I was twenty-five at this time.

I had just broken up with my boyfriend (I'm smiling inside because it was hard doing this, but I did). I was clearing my path of all that sought to block my success. New playmates and new playgrounds became my new motto! I didn't even know I had a disability, but I was so ready for change that I began looking at my life through the lens of inner transformation. Most people go through this during transitional times in their lives, and I believe these times are the most critical because they really show us what we're made of. I knew who my parents had raised me to be, and I was always one to be very true to myself. I knew early on that my goals were bigger than myself and that I couldn't accomplish them with people in my life that weren't going to be supportive and loving. Life is hard enough (disability or not) without difficult people who want to hold you back because of their own shortcomings or dysfunction. So I cleaned house and got myself ready to go back to school with no boyfriend or debris from my past to hold me back.

My first day at school proved to be an eye-opener. I had slept on my best friend's couch the night before, after having stayed up late consuming wine. I was wearing overalls and my hair was bushwhacked, so I just tied it up with a bandana (like a hairband) and off I went. I hadn't even remember that I had class that day. My best friend had heard me talk about it, and she had set her alarm to remind me. I walked into my history class that summer only to find that I was the last person to arrive. My professor greeted me with "Hello Ms. Hood, so glad you could finally join us." I found myself quickly making my way to my seat, trying to go unnoticed. In my mind I was thinking "Oh good god, this is going to be another Mrs. Killibrew experience, and I'm on his radar and I didn't even mean to be late."

Dr. Elchaig was a no-nonsense professor who prided himself on being the most difficult history professor in the entire college. (I found that out later that semester.) He announced the first class day that he would be giving us our first quiz the very next class day and that we were required to read our first chapter in order to pass it.

I came into my second class thinking I was prepared for the history quiz, but I only made a D. Damn. It took a lot of self-encouragement, but I kept telling myself that this was just an obstacle and that I couldn't quit! I made myself remember the rules. I kept going to Dr. Elchaig's class, and for the first time, I started to see patterns in the way a professor lectured. I noticed that he lectured in an outline form. I took down every single word he said and was able to recognize when he would change to the next talking point, which would prompt me to enter another topic on my sheet of notes.

I studied those notes word for word, memorized them. I went into my first major test one week later and came out with a B! EUREKA! There was hope! My study strategy had worked! I wrote down all my other notes just the same as I had done the first day and very quickly, test after test, my grade started to turn into an A. This one class experience gave me enough confidence and motivation to stay the course and so I did. I ended up taking Dr. Elchaig's class for my History I and II classes (which were required), and I made As in both. I was on to something with the note-taking aspect of college and ADHD, and I wasn't going to quit until I got what I came for.

This strategy with note taking was successful until I had a class in biology. I found that my biology professor pulled information out of her hat, and so the information she gave wasn't in the format that I had counted on in my history class. This was another glitch in my path. Their rules had changed but mine had not!

I attended biology class after biology class and eventually became reacquainted with a marine named Matt that I had known years earlier in the restaurant industry. Matt and I teamed up as study partners, and we found that helped us both to grasp concepts that we struggled with separately. I had found a blessing in a study partner and tutor and also another coping tool. I didn't do so well in this class though, because I struggled with organizing my notes and also with learning the material. The real problem was finding out where the professor pulled her information from that we used for studying on each test. I did OK on the homework but poorly on the tests, and I wasn't sure if this was because I just didn't like the material or if it was due to the professor's teaching style versus my learning style. So, I just kept on doing what I was doing. I was making real progress.

My job efforts during college were futile. I would end up losing forty jobs in fifteen years. The job losses would occur because I couldn't learn the job tasks fast enough (because of the way I learned) and so the employer would fire me.

Employers didn't have the patience with me that I needed, as I learned through repetition, and visual, hands-on and audial learning. I seemed to ask too many questions, which made the employers impatient, and eventually it always came to the same end result. These losses caused so much additional stress for me, but I continued, hoping the temporary agency I was employed with would overlook my weakness and put me into another job.

God has such a funny way of taking care of us, even within our weaknesses, because although I felt defeated in the job market, I was getting encouraged at school. I really tried to learn and perform for my employers, but I didn't know about developing coping skills, and I didn't want to divulge the fact that I was struggling. I only wished I would have had better coping skills or had been more educated about learning styles because I could have communicated that to those employers.

I would stay in the temporary job field for another five years, when I attempted to gain permanent employment with the state to lessen the load before I graduated. I found job environments to be one of two kinds. They either were places where unrealistic expectations of others were the norm (I worked for people who wanted things done yesterday); or I found the environments had no opportunity for advancement (at least not from the jobs I was placed into). Both situations created major frustration for me. I was growing disgusted with demanding people and my inability to fulfill my dreams. The limited pay within these jobs was attributed to the limited skills needed, and I wasn't being allowed to advance because I made careless mistakes in the details. Mistakes are what ADHD people are notorious for because we struggle with paying attention to detail.

People with ADD/ADHD either overlook the details or get overwhelmed by them. I still struggle with details in my jobs today. I have had to retrain my brain to take my time while doing tasks or projects that require detail. I also still struggle with information given to me in black type on a plain white sheet of paper. It's like my brain doesn't pick up all the information, and sometimes I transpose numbers or just completely overlook information that's needed. I have learned to make myself check and recheck my work diligently so that I pay better attention to detail. It's hard, but who doesn't love a challenge, right?

I'm interested in my current job, but it doesn't matter how hard I try, maybe I just wasn't made for details. God makes us all very different and there is a reason for that. I contribute by being an overview thinker, a visionary, one who sees the big picture. Or a leader! Visionaries, or overview people, need detail-oriented people to help them catch the details in life. I believe that is why we all need each other in this life, and I believe that half of society are detailed-oriented and the other half are like me in that they see the big picture! So maybe in reality I don't have anything wrong with me except that I learn differently! Wow, now that would be a concept. The reality is that sometimes the jobs that we're doing are not the jobs we were built to do, which can cause major frustration. Bottom line with this truth: God is probably using this frustration as a way to prod us into the right direction or down another path without us realizing.

I also struggle with the details in my own personal life, like putting up folded clothes when they come out of the dryer. I procrastinate and then when I get sick of the clothes lying around I will put them up and clean my room to create the order that I need. Order brings structure and when we don't take care of the details of our lives, or within our jobs or wherever, everything will feel out of order or chaotic. Details are critical, and we will have to master them to some degree in order to maintain any type of structure and normalcy in our lives.

I don't want to blame everything on ADHD, but again I am an "overview" person and a "big picture" thinker. I honestly don't care about the details of life unless they affect me personally. In the job market though, some fields require us to pay attention to the details, because when the details are left unattended they can affect the bottom line.

My advice is to pray and let God put you where He knows your gifts are! I know I'm not a failure, and I know that the gifts that God has placed within my life help me to do a lot of things very well. I just had to pick a field that I was interested in and one that didn't require me to really have to be a person I couldn't be at the level of ADHD that I was operating at. There are levels of ADD/ADHD growth, remember? Your brain matures and grows as you grow, and hopefully we are all getting wiser and moving toward higher levels of learning.

I took an interest test through Austin Community College that tested my personality and interests and matched them with jobs that I would be best suited for. The fields the test recommended were psychology, counseling, teaching, designing, the arts, and cooking. I liked all the fields the test identified, but the results posed a challenge for me because I still wasn't sure if these fields were fields that I wanted to do long-term. So, I just trusted God to keep moving me forward and let Him do the job of choosing for me and He did! He truly knows what we need to strengthen us (with ADHD or not) in this life in order to prepare and place the stepping stones that will take us to our real dreams.

I graduated in 1996 with a bachelor's degree in liberal studies from St. Edwards University. After graduation, I would go right back into administrative work, which I hated. Why do we do these things to ourselves? I hated desk jobs and there I was again in another one!

Interestingly enough, God had another plan for the little girl in second grade who had always daydreamed of being in the film industry.

This change would come in 2001, after 9/11, when I found myself getting laid off from working for a home builder. A lady I worked with knew I was very gifted in design and sewing and so she informed me of a costumer position in the theatrical costuming design field. (I had studied costuming in my undergrad degree.) This position would land me on the set of a film called *A Promise Kept*. This position led to many other opportunities to work in film.

I would get to work with such movie stars as Mimi Rogers (Tom Cruise's ex-wife who appeared in *Austin Powers*), Sean Patrick Flannery (*Boondock Saints*), Ryan Philippe (*Flags of Our Fathers*), Channing Tatum (*Dear John*), and Ciaran Hinds (*Tinker Tailor Solder Spy*) just to name a few. I had worked in live production on and off for seventeen years prior to working on film projects, donating my time at college productions and huge Christmas shows. I would be in the film industry for seven years. At the same time I worked as a costumer in film, I also worked as an administrative assistant so that I would always have income coming in if I didn't have a film project.

In the film industry you only work on a costume project for about a month to a month and a half, and then you might have to wait another three months until you get your next job. I didn't want to wait nor could I afford to wait so I would just switch back over to my administrative work and temp again between costuming jobs. In my film work, my ADHD wasn't a problem. Nobody in the film industry ever paid attention to my ticks and quirks. We were all odd ducks, and so I just fit right in! I was meeting and making friends with famous people and designers, and a lot of really cool doors were being opened up to me. Wow . . . I would often think back to Mrs. Johnson's class where I was reminded to stop daydreaming so that I could learn my times tables. I had never liked to attack hard things because I was always afraid that they would be too hard for me to learn or succeed at. The design field wasn't hard for me, and I noticed that my ADHD condition wasn't an issue as much as it was in other job fields. I was very gifted in the design field, and I still design things here and there. I sometimes toy with the idea of going back into film. It's kind of like buying a new car—once you get the itch, it doesn't go away until you do something about it. I just hated the inconsistency of the income and needed more structure to survive.

Too many interests can be a problem that ADD/ADHD people struggle with! I liked designing, modeling, the arts, political science, and biology, and I still do! However, I believe you can only focus on one thing at a time if you want to do it well. Once you have mastered it, you're free to move to something else that challenges you more. I believe you can be multitalented, but in order to utilize many talents effectively you have to develop and strengthen those talents at escalating levels so that you can utilize them at their highest potential. Just so you know, ADD/ADHD people have a tendency to get bored easily, and I believe that is why we have so many interests.

The film industry was the field I had landed in, but it wasn't where my true passion was. I was seeking that passion with diligence. My father wasn't there to catch me anymore, and I was at the age where I needed to get settled and find out what the heck I was put here to do. I believe that everybody has a destiny, and I just hadn't found mine yet, and this little glitch of having ADHD didn't help either. All of these things combined were minor mountains. They were hard, sometimes confusing, and sometimes they made me mad enough to push harder into the unknown. Had I not attacked these hard things, I would not have been ready for the major mountains I would climb trying to overcome this ADHD condition and push into my real destiny and passion.

My true passion would later be revealed as I got involved with a drug and alcohol ministry (over an eight-year timespan). This involvement would lead to serving and helping others overcome their own weaknesses. I found that as I poured into others, it would generate a drive within me to help them find Christ so that they could get whole and enter into their destiny.

THIS was what I was put here to do, and it was and still is fulfilling for me!

ADD/ADHD has been something—a big something—to try and master, and it still can drive me crazy at times. It's a condition that a lot of society has seemingly very little information about, especially how it affects learning. Honestly, I feel that the average learner takes so much for granted. Most of them just go through life never having to encounter half the crap that people with disabilities encounter. They don't experience the hindrances that we do because they have never had the glitches in their thinking to deal with. They don't have to cope with their brains not firing consistently or with the stop-and-start processes or the distractions (airplanes, flying saucers, or sudden noises, to name just a few). I'm not meaning to complain, I'm just making the point that their expectations of us are ridiculous at times. There is so much perfectionism in the world today, with so many people having unrealistic expectations of others that I think society creates its own chaos. So I refuse to accept their thinking that there is anything wrong with us (as ADD/ADHD people). I stand on the premise that there is something very wrong with having impossible expectations of one another! There are no two people alike on the planet, and that anybody would think it possible to force another into their own learning box astounds me. ADD/ADHD people learn differently. They think outside of the box!

We're not victims; we are overcomers! We overcome by learning the coping skills we need in order to progress and succeed.

I could have let all the job losses defeat me, but I didn't quit because I believed that my condition was serving a greater purpose. That purpose would drive me forward until I would start to see the light at the end of the tunnel—I was starting to succeed and learn. Besides, I couldn't quit because I needed a job and an education to survive so I just kept coming forward with God's help to try to understand how to beat ADHD. So be inspired and keep plugging away, because if I can do this so can you! There is no mountain too big and no obstacle too large. God truly makes a way where there is no way. We are not defeated! We are each brilliant students and adults with a wide range of talents and intelligence just waiting to burst forth so that we can become that next Einstein, or JFK, or the next Nobel Peace Prize winner.

We are each absolutely amazing! The way you think and learn is what enables you to see the world in a different light, and it is worth the challenge. So you can't quit or ever think about giving up because, who knows, if you do, you might have just missed the biggest miracle or career breakthrough that God was getting ready to show you. You never know when God is going to show up and perform miracles! So quitting school or life is not an option, and you need to make that one of your new rules!

Chapter 7

100 Pairs of Underwear

OK, I'm Kind of Rigid!

I don't know about you, but I hate doing laundry. I hate having to think about all of the details involved, the sorting process and which colors can be washed together and which can't. (ADHD people struggle with details, remember?) The thing that I hate most, though, is running out of clean underwear. This is a dilemma that I can never allow to occur. I've always been neurotic like that, especially when I was younger, so much so, that I was adamant about two things. I was adamant that my underwear was white and my tennis shoes clean and sparkly. Only those two things had to be that way, until I got older and my ticks expanded into other areas. (I say this cringing because I know it is quirky). Clean underwear is just something no human being should ever leave home without.

My underwear quirk dates back to early childhood. My father was late to work one morning and was trying to get my brother and me ready for school. My mom had already left for work and had been too busy the night before to do laundry. I certainly couldn't do it. I was only three feet tall and four years old, or I would have gladly made sure this task was "expeditiously" taken care of.

I sat there on the side of my bed contemplating what I was going to do because I knew that any minute my father was going to come marching down the hallway and tell me it was time to go. I wasn't going anywhere like this though. I was wearing my pair of shorts (underwearless underneath) and waiting on someone to come up with a game plan. I had already told them there was no clean underwear in my sock drawer. My father had just brushed it off saying, "Well . . . go grab another pair out of the hamper and use those until tonight when mom can do another load of laundry."

I think because I was short and the youngest that I was brushed off a lot, but today was different day because today was the "no clean underwear" day, which was inexcusable.

I was appalled. Surely they understood my plight and my need to have things "just so," so that I could function well in this world. Was it too much to ask? A simple pair of underwear?

My father whizzed by my door shouting "Melissa, I'm late and I need you to hop to! Seriously! I need you to get your things, Poot, because I've got to get to work." (Now mind you, I have no idea why he called me this name or his other pet name for me, Pooter Bill, both whimsical nonsense to me.) Despite the command, I hadn't budged off my bed. I sat there working myself into a quagmire about how I was going to settle this dilemma and somehow find a clean pair of skivvies to make it through my day with. My father flew past my door shouting but backed up in his tracks, back to my door. He stood there looking at me inquisitively. "Missy, what's the problem? Why aren't you moving because I NEED you to hurry?" The minute our eyes met this time I burst into tears because I just couldn't go to school like this with shorts and no underwear. I finally told him again of the problem, and he looked down and sighed.

My father ended up taking a dirty pair of my underwear and washing them in the kitchen sink with Tide. He then threw them into the dryer for ten minutes and, after much coaxing, convinced me that they were clean and so I put them on. He said after the first ten minutes in the dryer that they would have to air dry the rest of the way because we were late! To me, air drying was much better than dirty underwear any day, and we were on our way!

ADD/ADHD kids are kind of neurotic like this. We have certain ticks or quirks about the way that we do things, and when we are forced to navigate away from our schedule or routines, it throws us completely into a tailspin. I had my routine and I thrived on schedules. I depended on things staying the same so I could function in my little ADHD world. Why? Because schedules and routines create structure. Routine is a type of structure. But unfortunately for ADD/ADHD people, change is inevitable. In order to survive in this ever-changing world, we have to force ourselves to be moldable and pliable. As an

ADD/ADHD person, if one thing got out of sync, my whole world used to get thrown off kilter. It was that serious. To this day, I own at least a hundred pairs of underwear because of that experience. I have that many at all times to ensure that I never go through that experience again.

In my teenage years, I would move into different ticks or routines to have structure. It was a coping skill that I didn't even know I had implemented, but it helped me to get by.

So what are coping skills?

Coping skills are anything that the ADD/ADHD person puts into place to help their mind get through the day. There are healthy coping skills and unhealthy coping skills.

Healthy coping skills and tools include

1. **Highlighters:** Use colored highlighters to highlight pertinent points so that your brain can discern what topics to study. I knew when I was younger my brain had a very hard time sorting out information typed on a plain white sheet of paper. These highlighters were my way of solving that problem because the colors allowed my brain to see important information.

2. **Post-its:** Use colored Post-its. I use these to this day for the same purpose as highlighters. I can put these little stickies on my papers for school or work. I write special notes on them to trigger my brain to pay attention to that particular piece of information. I have used these so frequently that my brain automatically knows if there is a colored Post-it note on anything—it is usually important. (See picture on next page.)

The above photo is of my current work computer. There used to be over thirty colored Post-its on it. I just took down about fifteen because I no longer used the information. I usually have about thirty to thirty-five notes on it at a time so that I can function and do my job effectively—my computer is covered with them.

My brain knows that I have important information on each Post-it, and so it automatically looks for the color of the Post-it it associates with the specific detail it needs. I use this technique when I have a question about something at the office. I'm currently an office manager for my office, and I rely on this tool to help me with the "zillions" of details required to do my job.

3. **Calendars:** Use cell phone calendars with reminders and desk and wall calendars so that you always have

a visual cue for important dates and deadlines. Your cell phone calendar is one tool that you should never be without. The minute an important deadline comes up, I enter it on my phone, as well as on my desk calendar. This has saved my tail so many times that I can't tell you. Using your mobile or computer calendar should become second nature to you. Calendars help to implement structure and keep you on track. (Remember—we don't do well with details.) This tool will help you!

4. **Medications:** Do you take meds like Adderall or Ritalin? Set a calendar reminder (daily) to take your meds! They will help you to focus so that you can retain information.

5. **Environment:** When you have to study or do big projects, do you have a place that's quiet and away from uncontrolled distractions where you can stay focused? This will help you to be able to complete the task at hand. Is the lighting good? Or do the lights and sounds overstimulate your brain? The right environment is important when trying to study or do job tasks.

6. **Exercise:** Do you exercise? Exercise is a coping tool for stress; physical activity releases it. It also releases good endorphins into your brain that help you to focus. And it helps your health and weight. All this for about thirty minutes a day—how can you beat that?

7. **Study partners:** When you go into classroom settings are you able to discern the format the professor lectures

in? Do they lecture in an outline format or do they just pull information out of materials that they expect you to have read and retained?

This can be tough. You can overcome it by getting a study partner or by studying in study groups because other students might have the gift of teaching. These students might be able to help you more than your professor because their teaching styles may complement your learning styles.

8. **Office hours:** Students, do you utilize your professors' email or office times with questions about homework or assignments? Most professors that I have worked with are really good about meeting with students and answering emails. You can use these times and resources to ask questions without disrupting professors during class.

9. **Tutors:** Students, do you need additional help like tutoring or mentoring? Most universities have an Office of Disability Services (ODS) that requires that students be given additional help if they have a disability. I would utilize them from time to time when I couldn't find a study partner in a class.

There are also unhealthy coping tools that people utilize to help them make it through life. I say tools because any mechanism you use to cope with problems becomes a tool whether it's effective in the long run or not. That tool will either be successful in helping you to overcome or will be a self-defeating mechanism to drive you into deeper chaos. So what about those of you who have unhealthy coping tools as I know I used to have them?

What behaviors are considered unhealthy coping tools?

I know when I was younger, and sometimes even today, when I'm under tremendous amounts of stress, I just want to go and have a beer or a glass of wine. If I think about it though when the stress hits, it would probably be more beneficial for me to go for a powerwalk or run to release the anxiety and stress.

Stress and hyperactivity make a really bad combination for the ADD/ADHD person. Long-term consequences of these two can be lethal if left unchecked and cost a person their life through heart disease, hypertension, and other health issues.

The short-term effects can also be costly with legal fees due to DWI or DUI court costs. These court costs are usually incurred if a person is abusing prescription drugs, street drugs, or alcohol. Unhealthy coping skills keep you bound and are just not wise choices when it comes to ADD/ADHD. Think about it. Haven't we dealt with enough chaos in our lives? Why would we want to create more?

Don't get me wrong I love nothing more, when I'm not under stress, than to be with friends or family and have a drink socially. Balance, however, is the key in keeping the chaos away from our lives and usually for me (these days) I maintain that balance by just not drinking at all.

I know, call me "borrrrrring," but I guess I would just rather have peace and tranquility than the possibility of craziness or chaos. Bottom line: It all depends on what you value.

Chapter 8

SIMPLIFY! SIMPLIFY! SIMPLIFYING IS THE TICKET!

R iding a scooter at forty-six might seem odd to some, but it reminds me of being in Brazil or Italy, tooling down the backcountry roads. My retro scooter is perfect and practical for my life. It has a compartment on the back for my purse and books and is a wonderful gas saver. It only costs $7.00 to fill up and gets 280 miles per gallon, which beats the $40.00 a tank that my car would suck up. For me, the scooter is part of simplifying my world. Choosing to save a butt-load of gas money, even if I look goofy while trying to get around town, was an easy decision. I'm very practical and quirky already so it's not like my family would expect anything less from me. The whole scooter thing really didn't set them back too much. If anything it inspired them to do the things they desired whatever their age because none of us are limited by a number in this life. So be yourself and enjoy it!

I would fly an airplane, but putting me in a cockpit with all its switches (details!) probably isn't a safe combination. Umm . . . NOPE! I'm doing well to get on my blue scooter (with my navy pea coat and scarf) and fly safely down the road. I don't need to get myself into any situations while airborne.

Sometimes while driving my scooter, I worry that I won't be able to remember all its little gadgets, like the turn signal versus the horn or the brake. The other day, I was driving down the road, and I flicked my blinker button on (or so I thought) while coming up on a stop sign. You can't stop completely while turning or you have to deal with the whole "losing momentum" thing, and so I took off, with a lot more power than I intended, almost throwing myself off the back. You have to understand too, that the blinker button is right above the horn button. So as I go around this corner, I notice that on the sidewalk there is this teenage girl glaring at me. I was trying to cut off my blinker button when I accidentally hit the horn button (while flying past her) to which she responded by calling me expletives. Confused, I started thinking, "Did she just call me a bleeping blank?" I was like "By gosh—I'll turn this scooter around and go talk to your mother, you little . . . ." and "That's a bunch of Acapulaca!"—as my friend Susan would say. Then I'm thinking "Huh, horn, blinker, brake— which was that? Yes I do know how to drive this stinkin' thing!" I tried to make it sound convincing to divert myself from the offensive remark just hurled at me. This teenager's comment made me wish I had had one of those train horns on my scooter when I had driven by her. With my luck though, the horn would have been so loud, it would have caused me to crash or run up on the sidewalk into a tree. I finally concluded that the best response to the predicament was to "ix-nay the orn-hay and continue on my ourney-jay."

I was convinced to buy a train horn a week later though after seeing a man block this black woman in with his truck by an Auto Zone. She had apparently cut him off first, which had ticked him off, and so he just laid on his horn and scared the crap out of her and everyone for miles going both ways. It stunned everybody so much that traffic came to a complete standstill in all directions to see what was happening. This poor woman (at this point) got out of her car and started yelling "You blankety blank blank blank!!! You don't go and scare a black woman like that. I tell you, you blankety blank blank blank!!!" Man, the expletives were flying all over the place, and all the guy beside me could say was "Damn!" (I was thinking the same thing.) And yes, all of these stories in this book are true, but the names have been changed to protect the innocent . . . except mine. *Mi vida loca* . . . Spanish for "my crazy life" . . . ADHD or not.

OK! So where were we? I was going to talk about simplification. Simplification for ADD/ADHD people is important because when things are chaotic, ADD/ADHD folks have a real hard time focusing.

What do I mean by simplification? Well, to me this means creating the least amount of steps and details for your brain to have to remember.

Simplifying a school task

How do you simplify a school or work task? I use a few strategies, but let's focus on one. When I'm trying to memorize information for school or work, I use colored highlighters. I highlight the main points, and I memorize my notes by the color coding.

Here is an example of highlighted notes from a history class:

1776 Revolution (Main topic is highlighted in pink, or the color of your choosing.)

1. The Redcoats (Subtopic is highlighted in a different color.)

    They tried to hinder the Americans from fighting for their freedom.

    Paul Revere was pivotal in helping to warn the patriot fighters that the redcoats were coming.

2. States that they fought in (Subtopic)

    Maine, Boston, Rhode Island, Baltimore, etc.

Everything under the highlighted pink box has to do with the 1776 Revolution (main topic), so my brain will know that "pink" means everything about the 1776 Revolution. Your brain really will think like that because it's seeing the information as compartmentalized when it is in color. So you are memorizing the information in blocks, or blocks of color. Bottom line: this coping tool creates "simplification" for your brain, and you will memorize more information easier and faster.

Remember our brains don't do well with a lot of details. To simplify, I would count how many blocks of color I had to memorize. Say I had eight blocks of blue color (various subtopics), then my brain would know that I was going to have eight blocks of information to memorize about my one main, or pink, topic—the 1776 Revolution. Eight blocks of color are a lot easier to wrap my brain around than a sheet full of black-and-white information.

Simplifying a home task

Let's look at a second example of simplification. For this one, let's choose a home task. Say . . . laundry! I hate doing laundry, and I know that twice monthly (unless I have need) will streamline the process but be often enough to keep me supplied. I do my whites every two weeks and my darks/colors the other two weeks. Simplification! This might not work for everybody because some of you might do better with four times a month, I don't because I have too many others details that I have to keep up with. You do what works for you.

I'm telling you about simplifying because most of us don't do well with details or a lot of information, but if we can take school or job or home tasks and reduce them down to the least amount steps, we can remember them easily. So anything, any task, any schedule, any memorization for classes can be done if you simplify the steps.

Chapter 9

COPING WITH
A DIAGNOSIS
Finally, Answers

his journey with ADHD has been a long, hard road for me, as I'm sure it has been for many of you. My heart sincerely goes out to every one of you reading this. I hope that you have found what you have read helpful so far. I never thought in a million years that God would ever allow or help me to come this far, but he has. I find it very amusing that all along, while He was showing me all these things about my condition, I thought He was being compassionate in helping me. It was foolish of me to think like that because the Bible very clearly states that what God does for one, He will do for all. He did (and still is doing) this healing for me, so why wouldn't He already have started that work in you, as you are reading this book? I stand amazed at His tender loving kindness and even more amazed at His love that He shows us even in our own naivety.

In 1993, when I was diagnosed with this condition, I never dreamed of the journey it would take me on. I had struggled for so long before then that I had reconciled myself to the life I had, believing it was as good as life was going to get for me. But in 1993, I finally came to the point where I knew I needed professional help to find out what was wrong. I hated the idea, but I knew something was very wrong, and this "wrongness" was affecting every aspect of my life. It's only a shame that I found out about the condition after I was almost through with college instead of before.

My doctor's name was Dr. Theodore Daker. I had only been at my appointment for ten minutes when he asked, "Ms. Hood, would you ever consider taking a test to verify if you might have a learning disability?" I was crushed because I had never been told by an authority that anything was legitimately wrong with me, and so I had been able to discount all the speculation put forward by employers, teachers, boyfriends, etc. The speculation was easier to cope with than hearing Dr. Daker's question, because at least undiagnosed, the condition had a hiddenness and deniability that made me feel more acceptable. Several friends used to ask me all the time if I might have ADHD, and I would promptly tell them to "shut up" and that "a disability wasn't the problem." Frustration doesn't even describe what I felt when people would say these things to me in their attempts to make me question my fear. I could not wrap my head around what in the world was wrong with me, but Dr. Daker was trying to show me. Dr. Daker proposed a new option, and I had the choice of either staying where I was or accepting the new information, which would take me to a new place, a hard place, but a place that was beneficial to my future. I could have told Dr. Daker to take a hike, but I was so desperate for answers that I finally agreed that maybe there was a problem. I took the test for ADD/ADHD and went back two weeks later for my next appointment. Eureka! Dr. Daker had lots of answers for me. He started by asking me if I suffered from various symptoms. My eyes opened wider and wider, as I responded to each with a resounding "Yes! Yes I do!" The revelations in that hour were astounding, and his compassion and understanding were confirmations of what I had always dreaded: I was suffering from ADHD (Attention Deficit Hyperactivity Disorder). But at least now I had answers and a direction for finding possible solutions.

It's very hard on your heart to admit there is something wrong with you or something that others perceive as being wrong or out of place. I had been told all my life that I was "out of place" or "not performing up to standard" (except by my parents), and at this point I was sick of it.

Dr. Daker put me on Ritalin for adults. This prescription was later changed to Adderall, which I have done very well with up to the present. I wasn't very good at taking my meds at first, because of my own little secret rebellion against a diagnosis I didn't like. I realized in the end that the only person I was hurting was myself, so I made myself take the medicine to see what it could do for me. I noticed a difference in my ability to focus when I took the medicine as opposed to when I didn't. When I was off the medicine, my world went back to its usual chaotic mess. Yep! Medicine was the key so I stuck with it.

In my heart of hearts, I was determined to overcome this condition. Conditions are like the weather; they are subject to change. I also knew I served a God who had the power and authority over every "condition" in life, and I chose to believe what HE said about me. I made myself believe that I could actually have a future. My life was in the palm of His hands, and He knew the plans that He had for my life and that was to give me hope and a future.

I had suffered much depression with this condition. I had nowhere else to look but to Christ. The reality of having ADHD was depressing. I found it painful to have to admit the truth about myself, especially when it had been pointed out by others. I think I was ready for somebody to tell me something good about me so that for once I could accept myself.

You see, ADHD people have a tendency to be rigid and perfectionistic— things have to be done a certain way. This perfectionism even extends to our own person, our own vessel. I had such a hard time accepting this imperfection about myself, but maybe that was because of all the stigmas that went with having it. The condition was not in my plan, and it made me feel less than perfect. It had affected my self-esteem for years when I didn't even know I had it or what was bothering me. I made light of it in high school. I had been a blonde and had gotten by on the blonde joke thing, thinking that that would carry me. But the truth was that it used to bug the crap out of me when others would poke fun at my intelligence level. I knew

I wasn't stupid, and I grew weary of always feeling like I had to divert attention away from my difficulty learning in order to help save a job or to fit in, you name it.

The diagnosis was heavy to my heart, but I also knew that it's the heart of a person that matters, and people know when they are loved, truly loved, and truly accepted. I knew I needed change, and I was going to have to trust God to show me so that I could love me again. But the question was could He do it? I needed for God to change me from the inside out. I knew I was smart. Hidden somewhere in there under all the ticks and quirks was this person waiting to get out! Maybe that person had my brain, the brain that I was supposed to have gotten in heaven, instead of the one I got handed at birth?

I knew God had all the answers for me and that He would show me if I sought Him and so I set my face like flint and started asking and praying for answers. I took my meds because that was the only thing helping me to focus. I knew that I could do anything, and after that I made up my mind to see if God really did heal people.

The next eighteen years would prove to be grueling, but amazing, as I would find myself in this transformative process that would take me through a change like I had never experienced before. This process would show me what I was made of, and what I wasn't, and help me to distinguish God's truth about myself from what people had been pumping into my brain all the years before.

Joyce Meyer once said this plight in life "encompassed a Battlefield of the Mind" (Meyer, 2002, pp. 15–16). I had always heard that we needed to take our thoughts captive and start speaking the word of God instead of our fears back to our circumstances. We were supposed to do this because the word of God is alive, active, and sharper than any two-edged sword. It went out and accomplished what it set out to do. The Bible also said that in the beginning was the word, the word was with God, and the word was God—so I knew it had power! The last scripture that God gave me was that God promised to watch over His word to perform it. After having God give me these three truths, I put them in action.

Would they really work? Saying the Bible words out loud? What if I didn't know the word or scripture? (I thought this at the time.) And what if I didn't know what the heck they were talking about in how I should do that? I found myself quickly getting book after book from various ministries (Joyce Meyer, Dr. Mark Chironna, Chuck Pierce, Derek Prince), and at this point my brain was on overload.

I was also stressed out about trying to hold a job and fit into my job environments and learn this biblical material. To most, that would have put them over the edge, and they may have quit, but to me I didn't have any other choice.

In workplaces, my ticks and quirks seemed to get me fired faster than my inability to learn the job. But employers always judged me for one or the other. They couldn't seem to figure me out. This did a number on my self-esteem, and I became afraid of getting close to people. I found myself in survival mode just to make a living. I still struggle with getting close to people today—I think because I still struggle with a hidden fear of rejection. I was growing resentful. My dad was gone and there was nobody to help me. Nobody seemed to have the answers that I needed, and I was growing tired of reading books.

I still kept going to church because somehow the child within my heart knew that God wouldn't let me down.

Four years into this process I would start to see that the change was growing very obvious and that speaking the word over my life and brain was working. I would pray this prayer daily, which quoted two verses:

> *Lord, make me wise beyond my years and heal my mind.*
>
> The beginning of wisdom is this: Though it cost all you have, get understanding and wisdom (Proverbs 4:7, The New International Version).
>
> Then your light will break forth like the dawn, and your healing will quickly appear; then your righteousness will go before you, and the glory of the Lord will be your rear guard wisdom (Isaiah 58:8, The New International Version).

As I continued in this prayer, I found myself growing up in my emotions and thinking, which affected my cognitive abilities. I still had a few ticks and quirks (still do today) but nothing like I did when I first started. So I kept coming forward in my reading and in my learning the word of God. It was like I was trying to do three jobs at once. But somehow in the middle of all the craziness of this process, I found a blissful place where I didn't fight as much with the ADHD condition. I knew God was allowing me to go through the process, and instead of fighting it, I just focused on my learning and healing and doing what I thought He was telling me to do. That was primarily to focus on Him.

For nonbelievers, when you are hurting and in need of change, there is something very powerful you can do. The Bible says that if you will seek God or draw near Him, He will draw near to you. So if you are in need of healing, or change, or transformation, you have to seek Him out until you or your situation starts to transform!

I know this probably sounds like a lot of religious mumbo jumbo to many of you, but this process has profoundly changed my life, my perspective, and my self-image. In the end, I would do a complete one-eighty away from all the wounds I had received in my life due to ADHD. I would come into a place of wholeness. Let me be clear in saying that I have not been completely healed of the condition, but I want you to know that at forty-six years old, I'm still standing in faith and believing in what I know God can do for me. I'm almost completely healed, made whole, but my brain just needs a little more "tweaking."

I know some of you might be thinking "oh god—she's trying to cram religion down our throats as a solution to this problem." In reality, no, no I'm not. You can take the coping skills aspect of this book and apply those, and maybe that will be all you need to do and succeed in this life.

My prayer for you would be that if you are thinking that you might just need a little more help to cope with your condition or your life, then I can say that Christ is here to help you. He is here to help you make it through each day that you have to walk in this seemingly uncompassionate world that deems people like us "least likely to succeed." He is also here to show you that spiritual truths work. I'm here to tell you that you can do it your way, or His way, but I am a walking talking testimony that His way works and that the miracles are real!

He's a gentleman though, and He won't' force Himself on anyone. So the bottom line is that this conversation comes with an invitation, and that the choice to walk with Him and be helped by Him is solely up to you.

But as for me and my house—WE WILL SERVE THE LORD.

Chapter 10

THE TRUTH HURTS, BUT WE DO HAVE LIMITATIONS

It's hard to feel like you have limitations as a human being, but we do have them—every single one of us. I turned forty-six this year (the same age my father was when he passed away). I'm finding with each passing year that my body changes and becomes less able to perform like the spry, strong vessel it once was. I would have preferred to have traveled a road less rocky. My dreams would have taken me down a much different pathway than this one.

I'm very tender-hearted, and if I could have been born with wings on my back, maybe it would have been easier for me to have been an angel than a person. I have felt limited by the pitfalls created by ADHD as I walked my life. This has been no picnic, but I could have either focused on the negatives or seized the moment and popped my lemonade stand up and tried to make something good out it—made some lemonade. I choose to look at the positives of ADHD and of my life and to see the condition for the gift that it really is.

Did you know that Einstein had ADHD? So did the following people, just to name a few: JFK, Robert F. Kennedy, Ty Pennington, Steven Spielberg, Tom Cruise, Bruce Jenner, Prince Charles, Eisenhower, Churchill (my hero).

Many ADD/ADHD students have been made to feel that they were stupid, lazy, or ignorant. The people mentioned above, however, were far from being any of these labels. The stigmas are often given to those with disabilities when they are young because they don't perform like other people. To me, the people that make others feel this way are really the ones who are the lazy and ignorant. They are lazy and ignorant because they refuse to educate themselves about others, about disabilities, about how ADD/ADHD works.

People with ADD/ADHD are borderline, if not sheer, geniuses in that most would excel just as fast as anyone in education, if not faster if the proper tools were in place. So! Don't you go and believe everything you read or hear; the lies are just that—lies. Just because you don't fall into the mainstream of society doesn't mean you're not able to be somebody and do something huge in this life. I believe with all my heart that certain members of society have gotten very full of themselves in their attempts to make everyone fit into the same mold— their mold—for what they deem as "acceptable" or "normal."

What is "normal" anyway? Is the person normal who dresses just like everyone else? Is the person normal that learns like everyone else? I don't know, but what I do know, is that I refuse to allow anybody to label me or hinder my future. They do this because of their own lack of understanding. These people need to sit down with us and ask us about our days, and if they did, do you know what they would figure out? They would find out that although a lot of us diagnosed with this condition are quirky, and some of us might struggle, we like being us! I don't want to be like you or like anybody else in society. I only want to be like me! I love being me, and I love my quirkiness, and I love the fact that I can laugh at the curveballs thrown at me in life. I confess I could have done without a few of the ticks that come and go with this condition, but I love being me!

My point: learn to celebrate yourself and start to see you for the wonderful human being you really are, even with the condition. Don't ever let anyone dictate your future or your self-image. You are not who "others" say you are, you are who GOD says you are, and you are beautifully and wonderfully made in His image with His Love.

Those of us with ADD/ADHD often struggle with limitations early on if this condition isn't put into check with structure, good coping skills, or meds. In high school, there is a mandated structure of schedules and attendance. Most families also have a mandated structure established through the rules, regulations (curfews, etc.), and expectations for each child in that family.

When students leave these structured environments, they are thrown into an unknown sea and forced to create their own structure, which is part of the maturing process. Some students can do this better than others. Those with ADD/ADHD may come into these environments and struggle with focusing because of the stress of deadlines or personal circumstances, in addition to the stress of their ticks and quirks. This stress perpetuates the condition, which hinders their processing abilities and their maturity.

For those of you without ADD/ADHD, if your brain were getting interrupted all the time, you would be less able to focus on higher-level thinking too! It's the constant stopping and starting that disrupts learning. That is why it is essential for kids and students with ADD/ADHD to get on medicine when they are young so that they can progress and mature like any other student.

My limitations became magnified when I was under stress. Stress is the number one trigger of ADHD and causes my brain to overload if I don't apply coping tools until the stress diminishes. How do I cope when I'm under stress, or what do I do if I'm not on medicine?

Well, I make myself slow down so that I don't miss the details. The pressure to perform creates an unnecessary sense of stress. We're all just people and not robots. We can only do one thing at a time if we're going to do it well. I also have learned to make demanding people around me wait until I can help them. I'm not pressured by their selfish impatience when it comes to job tasks, schoolwork, etc. Multitasking is something that every single person struggles to do so I don't allow the unrealistic expectations of others to control me. NOR should you! I understand that you can't always do this when a professor or boss is hitting you with deadlines and other needs left and right. But you can get into the habit of putting those deadline alerts into your cell phone calendars, or desk or wall calendars, to remind you they are coming up. This preparation serves as a "visual cue," keeping the date in front of you so that your brain is constantly seeing it. This visual cue is also a form of repetitious learning. ADD/ADHD adults and students thrive on repetition, and so I utilize this tool whenever I can. I'm using it in this book by repeating information here and there, over and over again, so that you might retain it. Some readers might find my writing redundant, but there is a method to my madness!

I've also learned to give myself an ample amount of time to get work or assignments done. I have learned to be very diligent about prioritizing my time and sticking to a schedule. If my cell reminder says to start on a paper a week before it's due, I stick to that time schedule. This takes discipline, but you'll have less stress if you get things done early rather than wait until the night before they are due and do a poor job because you can't focus well under stress. Remember lack of focus is caused by stress, which triggers the symptoms of ADD/ADHD.

Stress in relationships is another topic that I want to talk about. I don't let other people put their stress on me. That misplacement is called "projecting" in the world of psychology. I have found over the years that because I tend to be laid back (believe it or not—when I'm not hyper—you get less hyper as you grow older), others will try to dump on me. This dumping creates unnecessary emotional stress for the ADD/ADHD person.

When I know someone wants to complain or just dump, I make this response: "Excuse me, I'm really busy"—even if I'm not. Some people are just "Negative Nellies" and I like being happy. Plus I don't let the dysfunction of others create more chaos in my world. I like to be around people that encourage me and motivate me with good things and not behaviors that drag me down. Yuck. I have found too that some people are angry because of where their own bad choices have landed them. Honestly, that's not my problem nor is it yours because none of us can live anyone else's life for them. We cannot force anyone to live like we would prefer them to, and if you try to, you will draw unwarranted stress around you that could have been avoided. I can only live my life and hope that I'm making a good impact on those around me who are observing my life and habits. Every single one of us is responsible for making good or bad choices that affect our long-term outcomes.

My only hope is that I get through this thing called "life" alive and that I am able to finish strong in the end. I am a truth person and being a literal personality with ADHD compels me to speak the truth. If the person trying to dump on me or project their anger on me won't accept the truth, then all I can do is excuse myself and move on. I know we all have hurts and issues, but there is a time and place for everything. If somebody isn't willing to do something about their situation, I don't want to be their dumping ground. I'm not the "Acapulaca girl" that everyone is allowed to dump on, but I will be your best cheerleader if you choose to come forward to learn and grow into healthier thinking. Remember that your choices will either bring tranquility into your life or chaos. You make your life what it is tomorrow by the choices you make today, including the people you choose to hang out with and allow to influence you.

Adjusting to new environments can be hard for those of us with ADD/ADHD. Some folks adjust to change better than others and faster. ADD/ADHD people don't like change because that means our routines are interrupted, which usually throws us off, and then we have to formulate new routines and schedules. My advice is to take a deep breath and realize that change is inevitable, but stress is optional. And change can be another opportunity to grow and enhance your skills. Remember to apply coping skills while establishing any new structure. Make sure too that you stay moldable and pliable and open to change. This will allow you not to be so fearful when semesters end or begin, or job moves come, or people come in and out of your life. Again, change is inevitable, but stress and depression are optional.

Change used to completely blow my entire world apart when I was younger. When I was a little girl, my brother and I were in nursery school together, but he was two years ahead of me, and when the time came for him to graduate to the first grade, the change overwhelmed me. He had moved on to elementary school, and I was stuck going to daycare without him. I was devastated and made up my mind to rebel against ever going back. My brother's advancement had thrown a complete monkey wrench in my spokes. I was used to his presence, and as an ADHD kid, I had a hard time with people seemingly leaving my life. So, I made up my mind just not to go back. It took my mom a week to convince me that my brother was not moving out, he was just moving up and on into a new grade level.

Change in relationships, sudden losses, traumas, or endings to relationships can be devastating to those who suffer with ADD/ADHD. It goes back to our reliance on routines and not being able to cope with changes. Change can be very hard in relationships, and support groups and counseling are sometimes necessary for those of us who don't deal well with it. We are human beings and so we love, and we get used to loving those people around us, but we must be able to let go of them, and "Let God in" if we are to grow. Any change poses a great threat to those with ADD/ADHD. Some of us fear failure so intensely that we rely on familiar people around us to feel safer. I need to let you in on a little secret though: we come into this world alone and we will be leaving it alone, answering to just one person. His name is Jesus. You don't have to fear the unknown without a loved one because God promises you that He never leaves you nor forsakes you.

I struggled with this fear for over forty years until two years ago when I almost had a major heart attack. I was awakened at 3:00 a.m. one morning with this horrible pain in the left portion of my chest running into my left arm and neck. The Lord told me (in my spirit) to call 911 immediately. I instead called the nurse at the hospital, and the nurse told me she was sending an ambulance to which I promptly declined. I didn't want to scare my mom, but by the time she got me to the hospital I was in so much pain I wished I had called for one.

The nurses rushed me to the ER, and the Lord immediately told me that this was going to look "major" but was going to come out "minor." The ER nurses gave me tons of morphine to ease the pain and then tried to get my vitals settled. I was admitted and finally taken into my room, where a nurse took my information. I had had a number of tests run on my heart, and they came back with high D-dimer result.

High D-dimer results are bad because they usually mean your heart is under duress, which means you're trying to have a heart attack. When my heart testing was done, and I was put in my own private room, and the nurse came in, I wasn't in much pain. She sat on the couch with her little rolling computer to enter my information for admittance.

She sat there in silence for about twenty seconds but kept looking at me inquisitively and inside I was wondering "What the heck is she doing?"

She then looked up at me and said, "WHO ARE YOU?!!" She said, "I've never felt this much peace in one place in my entire life. Really . . . who are you?"

I was very touched, but my response was simple. I smiled and said, "I follow Christ and have been in ministry for eighteen years while doing many other things on the side. But I try to be a Christian and serve Jesus."

She just shook her head in disbelief, and we talked about what had happened to me. She left about thirty minutes later when I started feeling the weighty presence of Christ in my room. For those of you who are nonbelievers, there is such a thing as the weighty presence of the Lord when He shows up around your vessel. His presence usually is so strong that if you were to be standing upright, you would fall down under the presence because your body just can't stand up under the spirit's weight.

I felt His presence (kind of like I'm starting to feel right now while writing), and then Jesus showed up in my hospital room. I could not see him with my natural eyes, but I knew in my heart that His spirit was there, especially when He started to talk to me. He said, "Missy, the number of your days are in My hand, and just like I protected you from being taken out tonight by the enemy, so shall I protect you all your days, and so shall it be unto you ALL that that entails."

I was so stunned, I sat there not knowing what to do next.

This limitation, the fear of death and being alone, had controlled me all my life, and in this very moment I was set free. His presence lifted, and I've never been afraid to die early or be alone since that time. My father and many of his relatives had died very early in their forties, but I knew that I would have long life. I have had peace about death ever since, and I don't worry about the future or what others say about it anymore. I am beautifully and wonderfully made in His image, and there is no mountain too high if He tells me to climb it, ADHD or not! God makes a way where there is no way.

Chapter 11

RELATIONSHIPS:
I'm Not Stupid, I Just Learn Differently

eing made to feel that I'm "stupid" when people around me fail to understand my learning style is one of the biggest irritants to me. I find it to be almost hysterical the way that society—professors, employers, even family members—has treated the majority of the learning disabled, thinking that they knew more about us than we did. Had our educators listened and really observed us, they would have figured out our learning needs instead of trying to force us into their learning molds. Education really is freedom, but many educators need to be educated about ADD/ADHD so that they will quit trying to put a square peg into a round hole.

I know in reality this ignorance isn't totally their fault as the science world is just now getting up to speed in their understanding of ADD/ADHD. My hopes are that this book will open up many, many eyes and allow, not only educators, but scientists and people diagnosed with the ADD/ADHD to better understand how to help and be helped.

It amuses me when I see people "think" that they have all the answers to my difficulty with learning. The true heroes of my life have been those teachers and professionals who had a gift of discernment. These educators had an innate sense that allowed them to see what I was lacking in my ability to learn and to help me by filling in the gaps so that I could actually enjoy learning.

My frustration didn't come only from most educators' lack of understanding, but also from the dysfunction caused by the condition (my brain not firing correctly when not on meds), which hindered my progress cognitively and emotionally. This misfiring held me back in many areas of my life. It hindered my ability to advance to the higher levels of critical thinking that would have allowed me to move into better paying jobs with more responsibilities. ADHD slowed my progress in my education as well. It normally takes a student four years to complete a BA, whereas it took me six years because of the stop-start thought processing caused by ADHD that interrupted my learning. My undergrad experience was so hard that it took me another fifteen years to get the courage to even want to go back to try to earn my master's.

I have had to push through self-esteem issues in order to believe that I was capable of advancing and moving up within education. "Stupid is as stupid does" was the phrase that Forest Gump used in the movie to label those who didn't perform the way that he thought they should.

I have come to the conclusion that I am no longer performing for anybody but God or Jesus (doing what He tells me to do), and I no longer have to struggle with what others think about me because of that truth. The Bible says that I am accepted into the beloved (flaws and all), and I am beautifully and wonderfully made. If God ain't stupid—neither am I! Nor are you! As a matter of fact, some of you are in honors classes and that means you are pretty intelligent. If you are not in honors classes, that just means we need to teach you how to implement better structure and create more order in your life.

People with ADD/ADHD are intelligent, and if the majority of them knew this truth, it would transform the paradigm for how far they are capable of advancing. The right coping tools with the right attitude could help anyone with ADD/ADHD to progress normally, if not faster than the average student. Many ADD/ADHD students who have been blessed to be raised within families with strong structure and parents who understood their learning needs are in honors classes. So the ADD/ADHD condition only requires having people around us who are educated enough to help meet our learning style needs and establish structure in our lives so that we can advance with ease.

Relating . . . relating for me has been tricky over the years. I feel that many people around me have wrongfully judged me for being (in their eyes) lazy, passive, or uninterested in advancing. In reality, my IQ is off the charts, and I am easily bored with mundane things and have desired a more challenging path. I love adventure, and my life, up to this point, has been filled with so much adventure and so many juts and sharp turns that nothing can measure up to the excitement it's brought me. I've had my moments when family would wrongfully judge me and question my own judgment, but I just kept trusting God with my future. I knew that He knew where He was taking me. My biggest pet peeve is when others make me feel like I have to explain myself or my actions. I feel that at forty-six years old, I've earned the right not to owe anybody an explanation for anything (unless it's illegal, offensive, or the IRS calling). So I don't explain myself anymore. I just continue on down my path, enjoying my life. I do try to keep all the "crazies" away from me. By crazies I mean those that would try to force me into their mold of being.

Relationships are important to me, but since my personality is full of ticks and quirks, I find that I have to guard against the nuts, fruits, and flakes. I feel that the majority of society has a tendency to fall into the mainstream, following everybody else's lead instead of celebrating their own uniqueness. In turn, this mindset also tries to force everyone into the same mold. Why would I want to be like everyone else when I was born to be like me? The same can be said for each of you reading this. I'm fun, hilariously funny if you get to know me. I'm warm and loving to those who love me for who I am. I am giving—giving is one of my favorite things to do. I give a gift to someone only to see their face light up with excitement. It's who I am, and each one of you reading this should celebrate who God made you to be. You shouldn't live constantly comparing yourself with others or trying to meet their dysfunctional standards because their standard might not be right for you. I understand that there are no perfect people in this life, but I know this one thing: relating is a choice, and we choose who we want to be in a relationship with. We should not allow others to be around us who choose to be abusive (emotionally, verbally, or physically). It's our decision. So why would anybody place themselves around these types? There are worse things in life than being lonely. Relating is a privilege. So choose your relationships wisely.

Relating for me these days consists of seeking out those who are like little treasure chests just waiting to be opened with the warm love of God bursting forth. The Bible said that in the end times we would know his true remnant by their love. I may not be perfect, but I love, and I've loved writing this book. Showing God's love to each of you has brought forth so much out of my heart.

Writing this book has been very healing for my heart. It has allowed me to finally express to others around me (like me) the pain, rejection, and the misunderstanding that I have experienced for over thirty-five years while trying to learn about this condition. My goal in writing this book was to show those diagnosed with ADD/ADHD that there are others out here who will love you unconditionally for who you are and for who you were born to be. I would say "flaws and all," but God doesn't make mistakes, or junk, in the way that He makes us. We are beautifully and wonderfully made in His image. And He's perfect in every way—especially in the way that He makes us!

Chapter 12

COMING INTO WHOLENESS
Accepting My ADHD as a Gift from the Lord

I would like to end this book by telling you Life is a gift. It can be hard, but it doesn't have to be. It's what you do with the challenges of life that will make or break you. You can either get bitter or you can get better with Christ. I understand that to some reading this book I might sound like, well, I don't know what I sound like, but I have a lot more living to do! I was angry while writing chapter 3 of this book because it reminded me of all the hell I went through unnecessarily at the hands of ignorant, selfish people.

Today though, I *choose* to see my condition as a blessing, a gift that God has shown me. The condition

102

has many advantages on many fronts in what it allows me to do.

I have advanced in my ability to learn to the point that I don't struggle with all the relationship issues that I once struggled with. I just avoid those types of personalities who want to control and hurt me because I know who I am now. I know who I am and whose I am—God's child. I make no bones about relating anymore. I don't try to change others, and I don't allow them to change me. People have a right to stay in their miserable dysfunction and that is their prerogative. I have also learned that I have the right to let these types go so that I can relate and thrive and be the person God intended for me to be with others who love me for me. The personalities I have gotten away from might not see me this way, but again, that's not my problem. I don't really care what they think anymore. The most important thing to my heart is being me and enjoying the life God gave me.

The other blessing that attaining healing and wholeness has brought is that cognitively and emotionally I have advanced to where I only take my meds when I'm under extreme stress. I have learned to deal with stress through exercise and my relationship with Christ. I usually only take my meds once or twice every two to five months. My brain still skips a beat here and there, but I recognize that and just continue right along in my journey. I am finally coming to a place of contentment.

The smartest person I have ever known told me as a kid: "Missy, there are always going to be people in this life that will not like you. You cannot make them like you nor love you (not even in your family). You just have to shake your boots off and move on down the road and don't let yourself get stuck there."

That was my dad's advice when I was in seventh grade.

The second smartest person I've ever known said: "Missy, don't forget to love the unlovelies in this life like Jesus loves them—remember that, OK honey?"

That was advice from my mom, and I still carry that advice with me even today.

The smartest person on the planet told me: "Little Flock, I am able to keep you, because your days are in the palm of My hand, and nothing can touch you without My permission first. I know the number of your days, and I have a wonderful plan for your life . . . trust Me in this!" That was what my Lord and Savior Jesus told me when He showed up that day in my hospital room.

So you see, I fear no one but Him anymore. I know that truth in my heart of hearts, and I want to convey that to each of you so that you too might know that He also loves you and wants to help and heal you.

You be blessed in this life and know that I love you, but more importantly so does Jesus! And He is REAL.

So with that, I would write "The End," but this is not the end for you. It is only the beginning as many of you move into your journey toward wholeness and success! You BE BLESSED!

Sources Cited

Meyer, Joyce. *Battlefield of the Mind: Winning the Battle in Your Mind.* Fenton: Warner Faith Publishing, 2002. 15–16. Web. 30 Dec. 2011.

Kaminski, P. L., Turnock, P. M., Rosen, L. A., and Laster, S. A. "Predictors of Academic Success among College Students with Attention Disorders." *Journal of College Counseling, 9,* 60–71.

NOTE FROM THE AUTHOR

Nothing in this life is worth having unless you know in your heart that you put some elbow grease into it. I'm a country kid, and I was blessed to have worked in the film industry and have one part of my dreams come true. I found out, however, that true fulfillment in this life comes from serving and blessing others. Being a blessing is my hope with this book. Thank you for taking the time to read my book, and may you succeed at every endeavor you set your heart and mind to.

Love in Christ,
Missy Hood

Printed in the USA
CPSIA information can be obtained
at www.ICGtesting.com
JSHW080001150824
68134JS00021B/2210

9 781630 474805